GLOSSARY OF
EPISTEMOLOGY/
PHILOSOPHY OF
SCIENCE

Jo Glorie
Series General Editor
c/o Paragon House Publishers
90 Fifth Avenue
New York, N.Y. 10011

Glossary of Cognitive Science
Charles E. M. Dunlop and James H. Fetzer

Glossary of Epistemology/Philosophy of Science
James H. Fetzer and Robert F. Almeder

Glossary of Semiotics
Vincent M. Colapietro

FORTHCOMING

Glossary of International Relations
Marie T. Henehan and John A. Vasquez

Glossary of Political Communication
Michael X. Delli Carpini

AUG 2 5 1994

A PARAGON HOUSE GLOSSARY
FOR RESEARCH, READING, AND WRITING

GLOSSARY OF EPISTEMOLOGY/ PHILOSOPHY OF SCIENCE

JAMES H. FETZER
ROBERT F. ALMEDER

PARAGON HOUSE
New York

First edition, 1993

Published in the United States by

Paragon House
90 Fifth Avenue
New York, N.Y. 10011

Library of Congress Cataloging-in-Publication Data

Fetzer, James H.
    Glossary of Epistemology : philosophy of science / James H.
Fetzer, Robert F. Almeder.
        p.   cm. — Paragon House glossaries for research, reading and
writing
    Includes bibliographical references and index.
    ISBN 1-55778-558-9 (hard). — ISBN 1-55778-559-7 (pbk.)
    1. Knowledge, Theory of—Dictionaries.   2. Science—Philos-
ophy—Dictionaries.   I. Almeder, Robert F.   II. Title.   III. Series.
BD150.F47   1993
121'.03—dc20   92-22762
                                                            CIP

Manufactured in the United States of America

Contents

To Howard Smokler

Preface

This glossary has been composed with the aim of providing assistance to students, teachers, and anyone else who wants to increase their comprehension of key concepts in epistemology and the philosophy of science. While these subjects are usually taught in different courses, they share a common concern with the nature of knowledge. *Epistemology,* which is also known as the theory of knowledge, pursues the investigation of the nature of what can be called "ordinary knowledge." The *philosophy of science,* by comparison, pursues the nature of what may be called "scientific knowledge." Although both disciplines are concerned with the nature of knowledge, specific courses with these titles frequently differ in their emphasis, as follows.

Courses in epistemology tend to emphasize the nature of knowledge involving objects and properties of daily life. Some of these will be particular (about specific objects and their properties, such as that this apple is red), while others may be general (about every object of some specific kind and their properties, such as that all MacIntosh apples are red). Courses in the philosophy of science tend to emphasize the nature of knowledge as it is discovered by means of scientific inquiries. Knowledge of this kind tends to assume the form of scientific theories (in physics, chemistry, biology, and so on), whose formulation often depends upon uses of language that are related to experience in somewhat more complex and indirect ways.

There are different kinds of glossaries, some of which attempt to be very "scholarly," while others are intended to be more "down to earth." This glossary definitely falls into the second category instead of the first. We have tried to produce a compendium of concepts that would be most beneficial for those who want to understand these fields as ongoing disciplines. Rather than attempt to trace the origins (or "etiology") of any of these notions, we have sought to present how they tend to be understood by scholars who are currently working on philosophical problems within these disciplines today. In every case, we have tried to give accurate reflections of how these concepts are properly understood today.

We have also introduced definitions for certain concepts that are not widely understood, even among professional philosophers, but that still appear to be important enough for us to include. These encompass various ideas about probability and explanation, for example, that ought to be generally disseminated rather than remain the prerogative of some limited group of scholars who are specialists on those problems. Moreover, we have tried to be selective rather than exhaustive by focusing attention on the most important ideas—the key concepts—of these fields. For anyone who wants to pursue these matters in greater detail, we have included a bibliography, which functions as an invitation to further study.

Before we had brought this projection to completion, we acquired a large number of debts to a small number of people. In his capacity as a referee for the publisher,

Wayne Davis of Georgetown University advanced an excellent set of recommendations for revision, the vast majority of which we have adopted. In her capacity as an editor for this series of glossaries, Jo Glorie of Paragon House provided outstanding advice on the form and formulation of specific entries, most of which we have followed. We have benefited from the suggestions of an anonymous referee as well. We are grateful to them for their splendid assistance, which has greatly enhanced our efforts. Anyone with further ideas for the improvement of this work is invited to correspond with the authors, who welcome your suggestions.

J. H. F. and R. F. A.

A

Abduction/abductive inference. In its strict sense, a mode of creative conjecture introduced by Peirce that does not qualify as a form of inference. In its looser sense, a species of inductive inference associated with Peirce that is also known as **inference to the best explanation,** this involves selecting one member from a set of alternative hypotheses as the alternative providing the best explanation of the available evidence. Hypotheses that explain more of the available relevant evidence are preferable to those that explain less. Those that are preferable when sufficient relevant evidence happens to be available are also acceptable. Hypotheses that are incompatible with the evidence are rejected as false. Hypotheses may be false even when they are acceptable, which makes inference of this kind fallible, but they remain the most rational among those alternatives under consideration. A difficulty that confronts inference of this kind is ensuring that every relevant alternative receives consideration. Other criteria that may affect abduction include relative degrees of simplicity and testability.

Abductivism. The view that scientific inquiries can only be successfully conducted by relying upon abductive principles of reasoning, especially the principle of inference to the best explanation. The abductivist model of science characterizes it as a process of puzzlement, speculation, adaptation, and explanation. This view is especially associated with the work of **Charles S. Peirce,** but features of this approach can be found in the work of Popper and others. See also **abduction/abductive inference.**

Abstractions/idealizations. The axioms and theorems of formal systems in *pure mathematics* make assertions about abstract entities that do not exist in space/ time (such as lines and points in Euclidean geometry). The truth or falsity of these hypotheses seems to be **analytic** and **a priori.** If those formal systems are provided an empirical interpretation and those entities are identified with things that may have instances in space/time (such as the paths of rays of light and their intersections), the results belong to *applied mathematics.* The truth or falsity of these hypotheses seems to be **synthetic** and **a posteriori.** Idealizations, by comparison, are special cases of physical phenomena that might or might not have any instances during the history of the world, such as frictionless planes and perfect spheres. These idealized entities may be useful in formulating generalizations that characterize the behavior that would be displayed under those idealized conditions. Alternatively, ideal cases are pure, illustrative, or perfect examples. See also **formal systems; mathematics, pure vs. applied; theories.**

Acceptance and rejection rules. Specify conditions under which *an hypothesis* (such as that the moon is made of green cheese) is properly accepted as true or rejected as false, or *a decision* (such as that we should go to the movies tonight) is adopted or not. Their application ordinarily presumes a set of alternative hypotheses in a specific language as well as specific evidence, in the case of inference, or a set of alternative actions and the probabilities and the utilities of their effects, in the case of decision.

Acceptance/rejection/suspense. The three possible outcomes of the application of acceptance and rejection rules. Acceptance involves taking an hypothesis to be true, while rejection involves taking an hypothesis to be false. When the conditions for acceptance or rejection are satisfied, hypotheses ought to be accepted or rejected accordingly. When those conditions are not satisfied (perhaps due to insufficient evidence), they ought to be left in suspense. See also **belief, doxastic; belief, dispositional.**

Action, rational. Any action that satisfies suitable standards with respect to the extent to which a person's actions tend to fulfill their goals. Various decision policies can be invoked to establish whether or not any specific action is rational, such as maximizing, satisficing and cost-benefit analyses. When numerical information concerning the probabilities and the utilities of alternative outcomes is available, the appropriate decision-making policy is often thought to be that of maximizing expected utility, where the choice of any action whose expected utility is not at least as great as that of any other qualifies as irrational. When numerical information is unavailable, other policies, such as maximizing maximum gain ("maximax gain") and minimizing maximum loss ("minimax loss"), among others, remain available and may apply instead. Behaviors that are not actions cannot qualify as rational (or irrational) but only as non-rational. Whether emotions can qualify as rational is largely an unresolved issue.

Actions. When "behavior" is understood to be bodily motion or other gestures (including the sounds we make), then actions tend to be restricted to behaviors that are intentional (deliberate) and to exclude behaviors that are involuntary (autonomic), although allowance must be made for the unintended consequences of intentional acts. Alternatively, behavior that is brought about by interaction of (some combination of) motives and beliefs. Alternatively, the term is employed in physics to describe the behavior of bodies under the influence of forces (as in Newton's laws of motion) or as work times time or as energy having a vectoral (directional) component.

Ad hoc/ad hocness/ad hoc hypotheses. Special assumptions (or measures thereof) intended for the specific inferential purpose of saving some hypothesis from refutation by observation or by experimentation. Unless those special assumptions can be justified (making them no longer ad hoc), their plausibility tends to be subjective. Alternatively, an ad hoc hypothesis is one that has no empirical support. See also **Duhem thesis.**

Agnostic/agnosticism. An advocate of the thesis that neither belief in the existence nor belief in the non-existence of God can be rationally justified. Hence, non-belief in the existence or in the non-existence of God, typically envisioned as a Supreme Being who created the world. Alternatively, anyone who is unwilling to commit themselves to believe or disbelieve something because there is not enough relevant evidence.

Analogy/analogical reasoning. Occurs when two things (or kinds of things) are compared and the inference is drawn that, because they share certain properties in common, they probably also share other properties. Because the first, x, possesses properties A, B, C, and D, for example, while the second, y, possesses properties A, B, and C, the inference is drawn that probably y possesses property D as well. The weight (or "force") of an analogy tends to depend upon the extent of the comparison and the relevance of the reference properties to the corresponding attribute. Reasoning by analogy tends to be fallacious when (1) there are more differences than similarities, (2) there are few but crucial differences, or (3) the existence of similar properties is assumed to be conclusive in establishing other similarities.

Analytic/synthetic distinction. Has typically been drawn between different kinds of hypotheses as possible objects of knowledge, where sentences are qualified as analytic when (1) their predicates are contained in their subjects; (2) they are logical truths or are reducible to logical truths when synonyms are substituted for synonyms; or else (3) their negations are contradictory. Other sentences are said to be synthetic. The history of this distinction is important enough to deserve discussion. Hume distinguished knowledge of *relations between ideas* (when one idea includes or excludes another; for example, the notion of being a bachelor includes the notion of being unmarried) from knowledge of *matters of fact* (where that is not the case; for example, the height, weight, and color of hair of a person who happens to be a bachelor are not included in the notion that he is a bachelor). Thus, knowledge of relations between ideas has been viewed as analytic, while knowledge of matters of fact has been viewed as synthetic. Similarly, Kant, who introduced these terms, distinguished knowledge of *conceptual connections* (when one concept is contained in another) as analytic and knowledge that is *informative about the world* as synthetic. While Kant asserted the existence of **synthetic a priori** knowledge that is both informative about the world and also knowable independently of experience due to the mode of function of the human mind, that position distinguishes specific forms of **rationalism** and has been rejected by all forms of **empiricism**. The analytic/synthetic distinction was a basic tenet of **logical positivism/logical empiricism**, where its defense was based upon differences between sentences whose truth or falsity can be established by purely deductive reasoning in relation to the specified vocabulary—including definitions—and grammar of a language alone. Sentences whose truth or falsity can be ascertained on the basis of these features of language alone are not only analytic but **a priori,** while those whose truth or falsity cannot be similarly ascertained are not only synthetic but also **a posteriori.** But the defensibility of the distinction itself has been challenged in an influential critique by **W. V. O. Quine.** Its status remains a matter of dispute within epistemology today.

Anomalies. Phenomena that cannot be explained or accommodated by currently accepted theories or prevailing paradigms in any fashion that is not ad hoc. According to **T. S. Kuhn,** an accepted theory or a prevailing paradigm should be abandoned for another theory or paradigm only when the new theory or paradigm improves upon the old by explaining the same old phenomena and at least some of the anomalies unexplained by the old one.

Anselm, Saint (1033–1109). Medieval philosopher and Archbishop of Canterbury, best known for advancing the *ontological argument* for the existence of God. If "God" is defined as that than which nothing greater can be conceived and if a thing's existence is greater than its non-existence, then God must exist (cannot not exist, necessarily), if Anselm's position is sound.

Anti-realism. The thesis that realism is false or, at least, that it is incapable of successful rational defense. See also **instrumentalism; realism.**

A priori/a posteriori distinction. A distinction between kinds of knowledge that can be acquired *independently of experience* (such as that 2 + 2 = 4 or that bachelors are unmarried) and that can be secured *only on* *the basis of experience* (such as that some apples are rotten or that John is a bachelor). Alternatively, the distinction can be drawn between beliefs and propositions whose truth can be discovered apart from **direct perception** or inferences based upon direct perception and those that cannot. Its defense requires a theory that supports this difference, typically one that is closely related to or else based upon the **analytic/synthetic distinction**.

Aquinas, St. Thomas (c. 1225–1274). A philosopher and great theologian who provided a synthesis of Aristotelian and Christian thought, he is perhaps best known for his "Five Ways." These are arguments for the existence of God. The first is an appeal to motion (or change), contending that there could be no motion (or change) if there were there no first motion (or initial change), itself brought about by an Unmoved Mover (or by an Unchanged Changer). The second is an appeal to causation, contending that there can be no sequence of causes and effects without a First Cause (or Uncaused Cause). The third is an appeal to contingency, contending that, if everything could not be, then there would be some time at which nothing exists, but since things exist, there must be something that is not contingent. The fourth involves an appeal to degrees of goodness (or of perfection) in the universe, contending that a highest degree of goodness (or of perfection) must exist. The fifth appeals to design (or purpose) in the universe, contending that there must be a Designer who imparts that design (or purpose) to the universe. In all of these cases, Aquinas closes his argument by making the assertion "and this is what all men call God."

Argument. A set of sentences that is divided into two parts, where one part (the *premises*) provides grounds, reasons, or evidence in support of the other (its *conclusion*).

Arguments are normally divided into those that are deductive, those that are inductive, and those that are fallacious. Arguments are ordinarily made in declarative sentences, which are used to make assertions and can qualify as either true or false. Phrases and expressions (known as "conclusion indicators") usually tell whether an argument in ordinary English is intended to be taken as deductive and conclusive ("therefore," "consequently," "it follows that") or as inductive and inconclusive ("probably," "it is likely that," "suggests that"), but usage is variable and does not provide a completely uniform guide.

Arguments, deductive. Conclusive, in the sense that their conclusions cannot be false when their premises are true. (When "All bachelors are rich" and "John is a bachelor" are true, "John is rich" cannot be false.) Such arguments are *valid* and their conclusions follow from them. But a valid argument may have a false conclusion if some of its premises are false. (When "All presidents are Democrats" and "Bush is a president" are the premises, "Bush is a Democrat" follows from them, but it remains false.) Valid deductive arguments whose premises are true are *sound*. The conclusion of a sound argument cannot be false, but it can be difficult—sometimes *very* difficult—to separate sound arguments from merely valid ones. An argument that is valid remains valid if other premises are added to it. Some arguments are fallacious even though they are sound when they beg the question by taking for granted something they are intended to prove.

Arguments, fallacious. Arguments whose premises fail to provide appropriate grounds, reasons, or evidence for accepting their conclusions. There are various kinds of fallacies. Some involve *problems of ambiguity* (where the same word occurs in the premises and the conclusion but with different meaning). Others hinge upon *failures of* *relevance* (where the content of the premises has little or nothing to do with the content of the conclusion). Still other fallacies arise when the premises are relevant to the conclusion, but are *not strong enough* to justify their acceptance, or when, while there is enough evidence, it turns out to be *unrepresentative.* The differences between "good" and "bad" arguments are studied in logic. See also **total evidence, requirement of;** and **uniform interpretation, requirement of.**

Arguments, inductive. Inconclusive, in the sense that their conclusions can still be false even if their premises are true. (Even when "Almost all bachelors are rich" and "John is a bachelor" are true, "John is rich," although thereby well supported, can still be false.) Inductive arguments are *proper* when their premises provide sufficient evidence for their conclusions, and proper inductive arguments with true premises are *correct.* A proper argument may not remain proper if other premises are added. The major difficulty confronting inductive reasoning is distinguishing inductively proper argument forms from others that are merely fallacious, that are deductive but invalid, or else are unacceptable on other grounds. Inductive arguments must satisfy the **requirement of total evidence.**

Aristotle (384–322 B.C.). A student of Plato who became one of the most important philosophers in history. He was the first formal logician, the first systematic biologist, and a great metaphysician and epistemologist. His account of what is known as *classical term logic* was regarded as virtually exhaustive of logic until the introduction of the sentential function in the work of Frege in the nineteenth century. Aristotle elaborated a conception of *unqualified scientific knowledge,* which is cast in the form of syllogisms in which the premises are prior to and better known than the conclusion, in which the premises are primary and indemonstrable, and in which the premises stand to the conclusion as cause to effect. This view thus reflects a special kind of **foundationalism** that arose from his commitment to essential properties. Aristotle's work spans the entire range of human knowledge, including psychology, ethics, politics, poetry, and aesthetics. See also **essentialism; explanation; laws; logic, classical term.**

Atheist/atheism. An advocate of the thesis that belief in the non-existence of God is rationally justified. Alternatively, those who believe that God does not exist, whether or not they have any good reasons.

B

Background knowledge. The beliefs that are accepted as true in relation to the conduct of an observation or an experiment, apart from any other assumptions about the relevant instruments, the antecedent conditions, and the outcome of the experiment itself. See also **Duhem thesis.**

Basic knowledge. See **knowledge, basic**.

Basic statement. Any sentence about the contents of specific, local regions of space and time accessible to experience. According to **Karl R. Popper,** the truth or falsity of basic statements must be decided by an agreement between scientific investigators, after which they can serve as evidence in testing empirical generalizations, especially lawlike ones. On other approaches toward understanding the nature of scientific knowledge, including especially various forms of **conventionalism** (or **instru-**

mentalism), the truth or falsity of empirical generalizations instead is what has to be decided by agreement between scientific investigators.

Bayesianism. A theory of knowledge maintaining that **Bayes's theorem** captures the fundamental principle of scientific reasoning. According to this view, adequate measures of evidential support must satisfy certain mathematical relationships characteristic of the calculus of probability. The cumulative influence of acquired evidence is determined by a process of **conditionalization.** Because these formal relations require interpretation to qualify as theories of knowledge, and many different interpretations are available, there are *logical* Bayesians (Rudolf Carnap and Jaakko Hintikka), *subjective* Bayesians (Leonard Savage and Bruno de Finetti), *empirical* Bayesians (**Wesley Salmon** and Roger Rosenkrantz), *critical* Bayesians, who hold to Bayesian principles but with reservations (Patrick Suppes and Richard Jeffrey), and *quasi*-Bayesians, whose differences from the others may be more important than their similarities (Isaac Levi and Abner Shimony). Philosophers of science who reject Bayesianism tend to favor **inductivism, deductivism,** or **abductivism.** Other alternatives include **orthodox statistical hypothesis testing.** Among epistemologists, Gilbert Harman favors inference to the best explanation and Keith Lehrer a coherence theory of knowledge, but neither is a Bayesian. Alternatives include different forms of foundationalism, internalism, externalism, etc.

Bayes's theorem. Derivable from the definition of conditional probability as a feature of the calculus of probability, where $P(h/e)$—the probability of hypothesis h, given evidence e — equals the product of the probability of evidence e, given hypothesis h (which is also known as a "likelihood") multiplied by the probability of hypothesis h divided by the probability of evidence e. That is, $P(h/e) = P(e/h) \cdot P(h)/P(e)$, where $P(h)$ and $P(e)$ are known as "unconditional" (or as absolute) probabilities, insofar as they are not formalized as "conditional" (or relative to) specific conditions. In order for the theorem (in this or more complex forms) to be applied, it is necessary to fix the values of the probabilities on the right-hand side to calculate the value of the probability on the left-hand side. The fashion in which this is supposed to be done is what divides species of **Bayesianism.** See also **probability, interpretations of.**

Belief. The state of accepting an hypothesis as true. Beliefs appear capable of variation in strength, where a person might hold some beliefs more strongly than others. Some quantitative theories supply a means for measuring the strength of beliefs, especially in terms of betting odds that one would accept under certain special conditions. The importance of beliefs arises because (1) we explain and predict events that occur during the course of the world's history on the basis of our beliefs, which thereby supply the foundation for our understanding of nature; and (2) we tend to act on the basis of our beliefs relative to the contexts in which we find ourselves, where these "contexts" consist of our other beliefs, our motives, our ethics, our abilities, and our capabilities. Alternatively, the state of accepting an hypothesis as true or as rationally worthy of adoption.

Belief, dispositional. A conception of the nature of beliefs as properties of persons. As dispositions, an individual's beliefs can be displayed by different kinds of behavior under different (possibly complex) conditions, and, when they are being displayed, those beliefs are said to be *occurrent*. Smith's belief that it is going to rain means, among other things, that if he has to go out and does not want to get wet, then if he has an umbrella but no raincoat then, unless other conditions inhibit him, he will take it along. Theories of beliefs as dispositions have been advanced by Gilbert Ryle, B. F. Skinner, and W. V. O. Quine, for example. Sophisticated functionalist views interpret beliefs as complex dispositions ("functions") relating stimuli, behavior, and other mental states, as in the case of D. M. Armstrong, among others.

Belief, doxastic and non-doxastic. (1) Any belief that at any time has been accepted by someone as true or as rational (doxastic belief) or any belief that, although not accepted by someone as true or as rational in the past, might yet be accepted by someone as true or as rational in the future (non-doxastic); or (2) any belief whose acceptance depends on the truth of other beliefs as premises to which it is deductively or inductively related (doxastic beliefs) or any belief whose acceptance does not depend on the truth of other beliefs (non-doxastic). Holistic theories of meaning and belief tend to deny the existence of non-doxastic beliefs in sense (2).

Belief, rational. Any belief that satisfies suitable standards of evidential support with respect to **acceptance/ rejection/suspense,** normally by satisfying appropriate acceptance and rejection rules. Various theories of rationality can be employed to establish whether or not any specific belief qualifies as rational according to that standard. But the criteria that establish the standard themselves stand in need of justification to be acceptable. The strongest conceptions of rational belief impose criteria of **deductive closure** (where, if z believes that p, then for any consequence q which follows from p, z believes that q), of **logical consistency** (where, if z believes that p, then z does not believe that not-p) and of *evidential support*, which may assume different forms depending upon the character of that specific theory (as Bayesian or non-Bayesian conceptions, etc.). Since these conditions are seldom satisfied by the ordinary beliefs of normal persons, some theories attempt to be less idealized and more realistic. They emphasize that persons can differ in their degree of **deductive closure** and in their degree of **logical consistency,** not to mention in their standards for acceptance and rejection of hypotheses, and nevertheless continue to qualify as rational in relation to their beliefs. Theories that tend to emphasize strong conditions also tend to be normative or prescriptive (in describing the criteria that are satisfied by ideal rational thinkers). Theories that tend to emphasize weaker conditions also tend to be descriptive or non-normative (in describing the criteria that are satisfied by ordinary human beings). The attitude that one adopts about these issues tends to distinguish traditional (normative) theories of knowledge from non-traditional (naturalized) theories of knowledge, including evolutionary epistemology. Epistemology itself is sometimes envisioned as the theory of rational belief. See also **action, rational; actions; belief; belief, dispositional; epistemology; epistemology, evolutionary; epistemology, naturalized.**

Berkeley, Bishop George (1685–1753). A bishop of the Church of England, he is best known for his phenomenalistic stance in maintaining that "*esse est percipi*" ("to be is to be perceived"), according to which nothing exists apart from its perception by some perceiving thing. Minds are therefore essential to the existence of things, which would pop into and out of existence were it not for some all-perceiving perceiver (God).

Brains in a vat. See **evil demon hypothesis.**

C

Calibration. Relative frequency of success in making predictions. A weather forecaster would be said to be *perfectly calibrated* when the proportion of cases in which he ascribes the probability x to an outcome A is equal to the proportion of As in those cases. When he predicts that it will rain with probability 0.33 over 300 cases, then that proportion would be $^{99}/_{300}$, were he perfectly calibrated. This concept occurs in relation to the problem of relating objective chances to our subjective expectations.

Category mistakes. When questions, especially philosophical questions, that require one kind of answer are given answers of another kind, a cateogory mistake occurs. The nature of truth, for example, apparently calls for an **ontic** (or **semantic**) analysis of the relation between a belief (or a sentence) and the world. An answer that appeals to **epistemic** (or pragmatic) considerations, such as the conditions under which something is believed to be true, commits a category mistake, since the question concerns what it means for something to be *true* rather than for something to be *believed to be true*. Things that are believed to be true might still be false. Some philosophical positions, such as **pragmatism**, maintain that positions such as this are not category mistakes but instead afford the most illuminating analysis. See also **ontic/ epistemic; pragmatism; truth, theories of.**

Causal relations. The relations that obtain between two events when one is the cause of the other. It is sometimes assumed that indeterminism implies non-causation; on other views, causal relations can be deterministic or indeterministic. Sentences that describe causal relations between events may occur in causal explanations.

Causation. A process or a relation by virtue of which one event brings about (or "produces") another. The producing event is known as the *cause* and the event produced as its *effect*. One of the most difficult concepts in epistemology and the philosophy of science, causes are usually assumed to be temporally prior to, as well as spatially contiguous with, their effects, where the occurrence of a cause makes its effect necessary (or probable). Although Newton's theory of gravitation appears to violate this concept by introducing action-at-a-distance, contemporary theories of gravitation appeal to the notion of gravitational waves propagated at finite velocities. According to Einstein's special theory of relativity, furthermore, no causal process can occur at a rate faster than that of the speed of light. Quantum mechanics poses puzzling phenomena that may or may not violate this assumption. The strongest conceptions of causation are those associated with **determinism,** according to which the same outcome is invariably produced as an effect when the same cause occurs ("same cause, same effect"). But this turns out to be the case only when causes are given descriptions that are nomically complete (by including a specification of the presence or the absence of every property whose presence or absence makes a difference to the occurrence of that outcome). Somewhat weaker conceptions of causation are associated with **indeterminism,** where one or another outcome in the same fixed set of possible outcomes occurs variably but with constant probability. Reconciling probability with causation has thus become one of the crucial problems of epistemology and philosophy of science. The relation of causation is typically contrasted with that of correlation, where it is widely recognized that correlation may be necessary but is surely not sufficient for causation. Classic Humean empiricism, however, attempts a reduction of causation to special kinds of correlation (constant conjunctions for universal laws, relative frequencies for statistical), but the success of this account has been widely disputed. The most important efforts to come to grips with this notion occur in relation to theories of explanation, interpretations of probability, and analyses of the nature of natural laws.

Certainty. The highest degree of confidence or the strongest kind of connection that is appropriate to a variety of different senses, including **logical, moral, personal, and physical certainty.** See also **doubt.**

Certainty, logical. Logical certainty characterizes things that cannot fail to be true because their descriptions are tautological or analytic. They are described by sentences that are incapable of being false (because they are logical truths or are reducible to logical truths by substituting synonyms for synonyms) or by arguments that are demonstrative (because their conclusions cannot be false provided that their premises are true). The sentence "Snow is white or it is not the case that snow is white," for example, is logically certain, given the usual logical interpretation of "or" and the satisfaction of the **requirement of a uniform interpretation.** That a conclusion is logically certain (cannot be false) provided its premises are true, however, affords no basis for assuming that those premises are true. Certainty in this sense is a logical property that can vary from one language to another but which is constant for every user of the same language.

Certainty, moral. The property a belief or a proposition is supposed to have when it is either necessarily true or necessarily false but neither logically certain nor physically certain—for example, that murder is wrong.

Alternatively, a standard of evidence or rational belief that is less than logical certainty but more than personal certainty. In resolving questions of conduct in courts of law, for example, the standard that must be satisfied to bring an indictment by a grand jury is *probable cause*. In civil actions, cases tend to be decided on the basis of a *preponderance of the evidence*. In criminal cases, the standard imposed is that guilt must be established *beyond a reasonable doubt* (or, "to a moral certainty"), which appears to be the highest standard that can reasonably be applied in courts of law.

Certainty, personal. Characterizes a person in relation to specific beliefs when those beliefs are regarded by him to be *indubitable* (or incapable of being doubted). Other beliefs might variously qualify as *credible* (capable of being believed) or as *incredible* (incapable of being believed). Certainty in this sense is a psychological property that can vary from person to person and from time to time. It is a very different property than rationality, since someone who believes everything might believe what he believes with a high degree of personal certainty, yet those beliefs would obviously have a low degree of rationality. See also **Bayesianism; belief; belief, rational; coherence; Descartes, René; doubt, Cartesian.**

Certainty, physical. Characterizes things that can fail to occur only by violating laws of nature (or descriptions of those things, in relation to sentences that either describe laws of nature or follow from them). If the fact that emeralds are green is a **law of nature,** then that any emerald ever observed in the past, the present, or the future will be green is a physical certainty. Whether or not this relationship between emeralds and their color *is* a law of nature, however, is another matter, since what we take to be the laws of nature varies from time to time in relation to scientific knowledge and relative to the available relevant evidence. An outcome is physically certain only if its nonoccurrence is physically impossible relative to the laws of nature rather than relative to what we believe to be the laws of nature. The relationship between logical certainty and physical certainty differs on various accounts, some of which permit logical certainties to qualify as physical certainties, while others deny it.

Ceteris paribus clauses. Clauses that assert, "other things being equal," which are meant to imply the absence of unusual (or interfering) conditions. They typically occur together with incomplete descriptions of the factors whose presence or absence brings about an outcome. Thus, ceteris paribus, striking a match will cause it to light (but not if the match is wet, there is insufficient oxygen present, or it is struck in a peculiar fashion).

Chance. Objective (or physical) probabilities, usually as understood on either the frequency or the propensity interpretations. Chances are objective properties of the world whose presence or absence does not depend upon the presence or absence of any minds, human or otherwise. See also **determinism/indeterminism; probability, interpretations of.**

Chance set-ups (also known as "experimental arrangements.") Any arrangement of objects or of properties upon which trials of some kind can be conducted. Matches that can be struck, dice that can be tossed, or coins that can be flipped might be chance set-ups. The extent to which they are completely specified tends to determine how reliably the results of any observations or experiments conducted with them—no matter whether these trails are natural or contrived—can be successfully predicted on the basis of corresponding laws. The phrase "chance set-up" typically refers to a set-up relative to which various outcomes can occur with various probabilities.

Chance, the fundmental question about. The phrase introduced by **Bas van Fraassen** to name the question, "How and why should beliefs about objective chance help to shape our expectations about what is going to happen?" The issue van Fraassen thereby raises is the connection that should obtain between objective chances and our subjective expectations. This problem reflects a gap between the actual frequencies that occur during the course of the world's history and the objective chances that obtain as features of the world's structure. Van Fraassen suggests that, even though we might be able to discover objective chances inductively, what we would really like to know for the purpose of making decisions is instead the actual frequencies with which events are going to occur.

Cognitive science. The study of the nature and laws of cognition in human beings, other animals, and inanimate machines, if such a thing is possible. The dominant paradigm within this field has been the computational conception, which assumes that human beings and digital computers operate according to the same principles, at some suitable level. The more recent connectionist conceptions of the brain as a neural network supply the foundation for alternative theories of cognition, which may afford new solutions to the nature of mind and the mind/body problem.

Cognitive significance. A property of a sentence or a proposition if it can properly be regarded as being *meaningful* (or as making a "significant assertion"). Both logical positivism and logical empiricism viewed the question of discovering the conditions under which a sentence is cognitively significant as crucial. This is a different question than when a sentence of a language should be regarded as being *scientific* (since some non-scientific sentences but no cognitively insignificant sentences could still be meaningful). Among the answers that have been proposed to solve this matter are that sentences are cognitively significant when they are either analytic or observation sentences or else are deducible from observation sentences (the criterion of **verifiability**) or their negations are deducible from observation sentences (the criterion of **falsifiability**) or both they and their negations are empirically testable (the criterion of **testability**). Solutions like these depend on the defensibility of both (1) the **analytic/synthetic distinction** and (2) the **observable/theoretical distinction,** which have been widely challenged. See also **demarcation, the problem of; meaningfulness, the problem of.**

Cognitive virtue. The capacity or disposition of a cognitive mechanism to be usually reliable in generating true rather than false beliefs under suitable conditions in relation to some specific domain of inquiry.

Coherence. A consistency requirement of sets of degrees of belief or of sets of beliefs that may be characterized in two substantially different ways. (1) Within Bayesian approaches that dispense with beliefs in favor of degrees of belief (or strengths of conviction), a person z's degrees of belief are coherent at any specific time when they satisfy the requirements of the calculus of probability. For example, if z believes that p to degree m, z must also believe not-p to degree equal to or less than $1 - m$. In this sense, coherence functions as a probabilistic consistency condition for a static set of beliefs. (2) With respect to non-Bayesian approachs that endorse beliefs about probabilities (based on inductive reasoning, for example) in lieu of degrees of belief, a person z's set of beliefs about probabilities is coherent so long as they are deductively consistent, where if z believes that the probability for an outcome of kind B under conditions of kind A equals m, then z must also believe that the probability for an outcome of kind non-B under conditions of kind A is equal to or less than $1 - m$. Either way, coherence functions as a requirement of consistency that is otherwise independent of coherence theories of justification or of truth. See also **Bayesianism; belief, rational; conditionalization; justification, coherence theories of; truth, coherence theory of.**

Coherence, strict. Imposes a further Bayesian condition that no non-analytic hypothesis may be assigned a probability that is equal to 1 or is equal to 0. This requirement is not a consistency condition but instead is imposed in order to allow z's degrees of belief in non-analytic hypotheses to change on the basis of accumulated information across time when using Bayes's theorem. See also **Bayesianism; coherence; conditionalization.**

Complete/completeness. A formal system is said to be complete when every sentence that is true of the abstract domain to which it is intended to apply (its "intended interpretation") is syntactically derivable as a theorem of that system. If it is also **sound,** then the properties of semantic entailment and of syntactic derivability turn out to coincide.

Concepts. What words stand for, signify, or mean. When different words are synonymous, they stand for the same concept. When sentences are synonymous, they may be said to stand for the same proposition.

Conceptual scheme. Any language, theory, or model can be called a conceptual scheme. This notion occurs with various shades of meaning in the work of **T. S. Kuhn** and others on the growth of scientific knowledge.

Conclusive reasons. In *logic* specifically: grounds, reasons, or evidence for a belief such that, if those grounds, reasons, or evidence are true, then that belief cannot be false. Valid deductive arguments provide conclusive reasons for their conclusions. In *epistemology* generally, grounds, reasons, or evidence for a belief such that, if those grounds, reasons, or evidence are true, then the truth of that belief is beyond reasonable doubt. That Lavoisier was beheaded thus provides a conclusive reason for believing that he is dead, even though "He was beheaded but he did not die" is not a logical contradiction. If all synthetic knowledge is fallible, it follows that there are no logically conclusive reasons for any synthetic belief, even those that are beyond reasonable doubt. Alternatively, the sort of reasons required, when the giving of reasons is necessary at all, for a person to be sufficiently justified in her belief to contend that she knows something. See also **fallibilism.**

Conditionalization. A process of changing degrees of belief under the influence of new information in accordance with (a special application of) Bayes's theorem. If "*Pn*" stands for the new probability distribution ("posterior" to or subsequent to the acquisition of some new information E) and "*Po*" stands for the old distribution ("prior" to the acquisition of that new information E), then according to the principle of conditionalization, $Pn(X) = Po(X/E) = Po(E/X) \cdot Po(X)/Po(E)$. Given this interpretation, Bayes's theorem functions as a dynamic requirement that must be satisfied by sets of beliefs as they change across time as opposed to its normal use as a static requirement of a set of beliefs at one time. See also **Bayesianism; Bayes's theorem.**

Conditionals. Sentences of "If . . . then _____" form, where the ". . ." sentence is known as the *antecedent* and the "_____" sentence as the *consequent*. While many kinds of conditionals occur in English, logicians focus on certain varieties in constructing models for understanding arguments. The simplest kind of conditional is the *material* or "truth-functional" conditional, where the truth or falsity of a sentence of this form depends exclusively upon the truth value of its components. When either the antecedent is false or the consequent is true, sentences of this kind are said to be true. A second kind of conditional is the *subjunctive* (or "were"/"would") conditional, which characterizes how things would be on the assumption that the antecedent were true. Thus, the sentences, "If this stick of dynamite were ignited, then it would explode," and "If this stick of dynamite were ignited, then it would not explode," as material conditionals, might both be true as long as their antecedents are false. But as subjunctive conditionals, they cannot both be true, since they characterize different ways things would be on the assumption that their antecedents are true. Subjunctives with false antecedents are often called *counterfactual* conditionals. Among various kinds of conditionals that are also studied by philosophers of science are causal conditionals, nomic conditionals, and various probabilistic conditionals. These are "non-truth-functional" because their truth or falsity depends on other factors beyond the truth value of their antecedents and consequents. Some theoreticians view lawlike sentences as subjunctive generalizations, while others prefer to view them as material generalizations that satisfy special pragmatic conditions. Connections between subjunctives, dispositions, and lawlike sentences have been explored by **Karl R. Popper, Nelson Goodman,** and **David Lewis,** among others. See also **laws of nature.**

Conditionals, causal. Any conditional based upon a causal connection between the antecedent and the consequent. The theory of conditionals of this kind presupposes an analysis of causal relations. Some theories draw distinctions between causal conditionals of *universal strength* (where the same outcome occurs in every case without exception) and those of *probabilistic strength* (where one or another outcome within a fixed set of possible outcomes occurs in every case with a certain probability), a conception that is fundamental to the interpretation of probability as a propensity. See also **causation; conditionals; probability, propensity interpretation of.**

Conditionals, counterfactual. See also **conditionals.**

Conditionals, extensional. Any conditional whose truth value depends only on the truth values of its antecedent and its consequent without regard for the existence of any logical, causal, nomic, or other relation between them. Hence, any material conditional in truth-functional logic.

Conditionals, intensional. Any conditional whose truth value does not depend only upon the truth values of its antecedent and its consequent but upon the existence of some logical, causal, nomic, or other relation between them.

Conditionals, subjunctive. See also **conditionals.**

Conditions, necessary. Conditions in the absence of which nothing would be a thing of the specified kind. Something can be a fifty-dollar bill, for example, only if it is printed on paper; hence, being printed on paper is a necessary condition for being a fifty-dollar bill.

Conditions of knowledge. Any necessary or sufficient conditions for the possession of knowledge. The standard conception, for example, asserts that three conditions must be satisfied for any person z to know that p, namely: when (1) z believes that p, (2) z has appropriate evidence to believe that p, and (3) it is the case that p. The first is a belief condition, the second is a warrant condition, and the third is a truth condition. Hence, on the standard conception, the satisfaction of each of these conditions is necessary and their combined satisfaction is sufficient for person z to know that p, because knowledge is warranted, true belief. Various theories differ in their necessary and sufficient conditions for knowledge.

Conditions of truth. See also **truth conditions.**

Conditions, sufficient. Conditions in the presence of which a thing would be a thing of the specified kind. Anything that is a freshman, for example, is a student; hence, being a freshman is a sufficient condition for being a student.

Confirmation, degrees of. Numerical measures of the evidential support that different kinds and amounts of evidence provide to different hypotheses or theories. See also **confirmation, theories of.**

Confirmation, paradoxes of. A conflict of intuitions about confirmation that is difficult to explain, which arises when two intuitively appealing conceptions are combined, namely: (1) the idea that lawlike sentences as universal generalizations of material (or truth-functional) conditionals are *confirmed* by instances of their antecedents that also satisfy their consequents; *disconfirmed* by instances of their antecedents that fail to satisfy their consequents; and *neither* confirmed *nor* disconfirmed by instances that fail to satisfy their antecedents (which Hempel has referred to as "Nicod's criterion"); and (2) the idea that materially equivalent sentences are confirmed or disconfirmed by exactly the same evidence. The universal generalization, "All ravens are black," for example, is equivalent to the generalization, "All non-black things are non-ravens," and therefore ought to be confirmed and disconfirmed in accordance with Nicod's criterion by exactly the same evidence. Yet, while a yellow cow or a red leaf would confirm "All non-black things are non-ravens," it is not obvious that this evidence should confirm, "All crows are black," even though these hypotheses are materially equivalent. This problem has generated a voluminous literature. Hempel has persisted in the view that the sense of paradox attending these conditions is purely psychological, but other authors have suggested alternative explanations, including the view that lawlike sentences cannot be adequately formalized as extensional generalizations. See also **conditionals, subjunctive; laws; lawlike sentences.**

Confirmation, theories of. Theories for measuring the support that given evidence confers upon various hypotheses. Alternatively, a theory of confirmation is a theory of inductive inference. The dominant theories of confirmation at present are ones based on **Bayes's theorem, likelihoods,** and **orthodox statistical hypothesis testing.**

Confirmation vs. truth. Evidence that confirms an hypothesis does not thereby guarantee its truth. Truth appears to be a relation between language and the world, where a sentence is true when what that sentence asserts to be the case is the case. But a sentence can be confirmed even if it is false and can be true even if it is never confirmed. The hypothesis of the existence of intelligent life elsewhere in the universe may be true, yet remain unconfirmed. Newtonian mechanics was among the best confirmed theories in science, yet it no longer appears to be true. Truth is a semantic (or **ontic**) concept, but confirmation is a pragmatic (or **epistemic**) concept. For theories, such as coherence theories, that reject more traditional conceptions of truth, belief sets that satisfy specific

27

relations of coherence among themselves, in particular, may either be viewed as confirmed or as true (or both).

Conjectures and refutations. A methodology for the discovery of scientific knowledge advocated by **Karl R. Popper.** According to Popper, induction cannot sustain the discovery of laws and theories, but lawlike hypotheses can still be subjected to severe tests by attempting to refute them. Those that withstand our best efforts to show that they are false are our best guesses about what is true. However, that they have withstood our best efforts to refute them provides no guarantee of truth, because we may have not yet discovered how to refute them. Because our best guesses have more content than our evidence, Popper's rejection of "induction" should be understood as directed toward induction by simple enumeration and various probabilistic measures of evidential support rather than as a rejection of ampliative inference. See also **demarcation, the problem of; falsifiability; Popper, Karl R.**

Conjunctivitis. A difficulty that arises with probabilistic acceptance rules because the probability of a conjunction of two or more hypotheses must be equal to or lower than the probability for any of them individually. Although this mathematical property follows from the multiplication axiom of probability, the problem requires probabilistic acceptance rules. In application to contingent, empirical generalizations, whose individual conjuncts have probabilities that are less than one, the probability of an unrestricted generalization, especially, which is logically equivalent to a material conjunction of infinite length (but also including **lawlike sentences**), cannot exceed zero. If the evidential support for an hypothesis to be accepted must exceed some specific value, such as 0.5, then no such hypothesis can ever be accepted.

(This differs from the lottery paradox.) Some thinkers want to preserve probabilistic acceptance rules but tinker with the values that lawlike hypotheses can acquire, while other thinkers dispense with probabilistic acceptance rules altogether. The problem was first noted by Henry Kyburg, Jr.

Consequences. (1) The *logical* consequences of a sentence (or belief) consist of the other sentences (or beliefs) that must be true if the sentence (or belief) is true. They are implied by those sentences (or beliefs). (2) The *causal* consequences of an event (or a state of affairs) consist of all the other events (or states of affairs) that must occur if that event (or state of affairs) occurs. They are effects of those events (or states) as their causes.

Constant conjunctions. See **causation; empiricism, Humean; laws of nature, regularity theory of.**

Context of discovery/context of justification. A distinction between the invention or discovery of an idea (hypothesis or theory) and the acceptance or evaluation of that idea (hypothesis or theory). It has widely been assumed that invention or discovery is exclusively psychological, where the principles of logic do not apply, while acceptance or evaluation is a logical activity, where psychological considerations have no weight. Rules of thumb that are sometimes helpful but have exceptions in coming up with new ideas are known as *heuristics*, but heuristics are normally not viewed as providing a logic of discovery. Were there any general principles of discovery or invention, then they would qualify as a logic of discovery, the existence of which remains a matter of debate. Those who discuss this issue include **Reichenbach, Salmon,** and **Hanson.**

Contradictory sentences. Pairs of sentences so related that they cannot both be true and they cannot both be false. Thus, assuming the existence of at least some men, the hypotheses that all men are mortal and that some men are not mortal cannot both be true and cannot both be false: Exactly one of them has to be true. *Contraries* are sentences that cannot both be true but can both be false. That all men are mortal and that no men are mortal cannot both be true but can both be false, if some men are mortal while some are not. See also **sentences/statements.**

Contrary sentences. See **contradictory sentences.**

Conventionalism. The view that, although truth or falsity are properties of sentences about the content of our immediate experience, they cannot be properly viewed as properties of sentences that transcend the content of immediate experience. Thus, the truth or falsity of sentences that assert lawlike hypotheses or scientific theories have to be decided by agreement among the members of the community of inquirers, especially by scientific investigators. This position is usually defended on the basis of the **observable/theoretical distinction** by accepting the significance of observational sentences but denying it to theoretical ones.

Corroboration. Any serious but unsuccessful attempt to show that an hypothesis or theory is false qualifies as evidence that corroborates it. The theory of corroboration has been developed especially in the work of **Karl R. Popper,** who has been widely viewed as a champion of **deductivism.** It is important to note, however, that corroboration is a form of inductive inference, where any hypothesis or theory, no matter how strongly corroborated, might turn out to be false. See also **conjectures and refutations.**

Counterexamples. Examples which violate an hypothesis, especially in philosophical discourse. The claim that it is morally wrong to lie, for example, could be rebutted by the case of a spy who, were he to identify his collaborators, would contribute to bringing about their capture and death. When a generalization such as this one, which properly functions as a "rule of thumb" that is normally correct but nevertheless has some exceptions (as this counterexample displays), is treated as though it had no exceptions, then what is known as the fallacy of accident is committed.

Counterexamples, Gettier-style. Examples that are alleged to undermine or are often thought to violate the traditional conception of knowledge by demonstrating that beliefs that are both warranted and true are nevertheless not invariably properly viewed as cases of knowledge. Typically, these examples depend on the following elements: (1) a person z believes that p on the basis of what seems to be appropriate (perceptual) evidence; (2) from the belief that p, z infers (deductively) that p-or-q; where (3) as it happens, p-or-q is true but only because q is true, since p turns out to be false. As a result, z's belief in p-or-q is both warranted and true. Thus, on the traditional conception, it should qualify as knowledge. Since the evidence upon which that belief is based includes a false belief, however, it does not appear to properly qualify as knowledge. If beliefs based upon perception could not be false, of course, Gettier-style counterexamples of this specific form could never arise. But others involving induction, where a person z infers (inductively) that p on the basis of appropriate evidence and, from her belief that p, z infers (deductively) that p-or-q (and again p turns out to be false), can supply another class of counterexamples. One solution to this difficulty appears to be to insist that a true warranted belief cannot qualify as "knowledge" unless every belief that warrants that belief is true. Another is to accept their force as

31

counterexamples to the traditional conception and to adopt an alternative conception of knowledge.

Counterfactual conditionals. See also **conditionals, counterfactual.**

Covering law. Any lawlike premise that appears in an explanation where the phenomenon to be explained is subsumed as an instance of the law. See also **explanation; explanation, covering-law model of.**

Criteria, the problem of. Indicates the difficulty we confront when we want to distinguish between the things we know and the things we do not know. In order to accomplish this task, we need multiple criteria (or a single criterion) to distinguish cases of knowledge from cases of other-than-knowledge. To devise those criteria (or that criterion), however, we have to be able to already tell which cases are and which are not cases of knowledge, in which case we do not need those criteria (or that criterion), after all. Alternatively, the fundamental problem confronting **epistemology** is that at any specific time we have no way to distinguish warranted beliefs that are true from warranted beliefs that are false. The solution appears to depend upon evidential indicators that may change across time, yet we remain in the situation of still being unable to distinguish at any later time then-warranted beliefs that are true from then-warranted beliefs that are false. Thus, we may be rationally obligated to believe things that are false. The evidence initially available indicated that Oswald alone killed Kennedy, but more recent evidence suggests that a conspiracy existed. Those beliefs may be rational, given different evidence, but both cannot be true.

Criterion/definition distinction. The epistemic criterion that is employed to infer that something is a thing of a certain kind ordinarily differs from what it is to be a thing of that kind. IQ tests, for example, can be used as a basis for classifying persons, but those scores are only fallible evidence about a person's intelligence. Definitions define properties, but the satisfaction of criteria is used to indicate their presence.

Crucial experiments. Any observations or experiments that provide the opportunity to decisively establish the truth or falsity of alternative hypotheses or theories are referred to as "crucial experiments." Perhaps the most celebrated example in history is Arthur Eddington's measurement of the influence of gravitational attraction on light during a 1919 eclipse, confirming Einstein's theory while disconfirming Newton's. The **Duhem thesis** suggests that the existence of crucial experiments is problematical.

D

Data domain. The observations and experiments that can be conducted in relation to a fixed set of instruments and technology. This notion was introduced by Robert Ackermann.

Decision. The process of selecting a course of action when several alternatives are available in relation to different possible states of the world. When the actual state of the world is known, a decison is said to be made under *conditions of certainty*. When the probabilities of various states of the world are known, a decision is said to be made under *conditions of risk*. When neither the actual state of the world nor the probabilities of various states of the world are known, it is said to be made under *conditions of uncertainty*. See also **decision vs. inference.**

Decision vs. inference. Deciding what course of action to adopt and inferring what hypotheses or theories to accept appear to be very different kinds of activities. Decisions are typically made on the basis of the then-available evidence relative to a limited set of alternatives. Once made, decisions often cannot be taken back. Inferences are typically made based upon the available evidence relative to a limited set of alternatives, too, but where later observations and experiments can change the evidence that is available and further reflection can change the set of alternatives. The distinction between them, however, is not entirely clear-cut, insofar as *deciding that* appears to involve inference whereas *deciding to* does not. See also **acceptance and rejection rules.**

Deductive closure. A set is said to be deductively closed when every logical consequence of the members of a set is also a member of that set. The deductive closure of a set S is the union of S with the set of logical consequences that follow from S. This condition is frequently adopted as a necessary condition for rationality of belief. Thus, if z believes that p and q follow from p, then z should believe that q as well. Such a condition appears to be appropriate, since presumably z ought to believe anything that has to be true as a consequence of believing that something is true, but it has been criticized as too strong to be justifiable, especially by proponents of naturalized epistemology. See also **consequences; logical consistency; naturalized epistemology.**

Deductivism. The view that scientific inquiries can be successfully conducted by relying exclusively upon deductive principles of reasoning. The deductivist model of science characterizes it as a process of conjecture, derivation, experimentation, and elimination, where the basic principle of reasoning is deduction by **modus tollens.**

Although this view is usually associated with Popper, his rejection of induction should be understood to apply in the narrow senses of induction by enumeration and of probabilistic conceptions of confirmation, especially Bayesian, rather than as a rejection of induction in the broader sense of ampliative inference, where an inference is *ampliative* when its conclusion has more content than (or "goes beyond") its premises. Popper acknowledges that we should depend on our best tested theories in anticipating the course of future experience, while emphasizing that those theories we depend upon are by no means guaranteed to be true and may eventually be discovered to be false. Alternatively, deductivism is the advocacy of deductive methods to the exclusion of alternative methods within any domain of inquiry.

Defeasibility. That property of a belief that renders it capable of being rebutted or defeated by the existence of at least one true proposition, where, if that proposition were added to the beliefs justifying that belief, then its acceptance would no longer be warranted. Alternatively, beliefs are said to be "defeasible" when they are capable of being defeated on the basis of forms of evidence that are publicly accessible (or intersubjective).

Defined terms/primitive terms. See also **definitions.**

Definite descriptions. A phrase or description beginning with the word "the" that applies to one and only one thing by implicitly asserting that there exists at least one such thing and that there exists at most one such thing. Bertrand Russell proposed definite descriptions as the proper way to understand singular reference. An example that he discussed was "the author of *Waverley*," where *Waverley* was a novel whose authorship was at the time unknown. Speculation had it that Sir Walter Scott was the author of *Waverley*, which Russell took to be true if and only if there was at least one author of *Waverley*, there was at most one author of *Waverley*, and that person was identical with Scott.

Definitions. Explanations of the meaning of words using other words. They are linguistic entities that have two linguistic parts, a *definiendum*, which consists of the word, phrase, or expression to be defined, and a *definiens*, which is some word, phrase, or expression by means of which it is defined. A standard symbol for displaying a definition is ". . . = df _____," which means ". . . means by definition _____." Every word can be defined within a language only on pain of an infinite regress (whereby new words are introduced to explain the meaning of old words, and newer words to explain their meaning in turn, ad infinitum) or of vicious circularity (where a word is explained by means of other words that are ultimately explained by means of that original word). It is apparently futile to attempt to explain the meaning of every word in a language while remaining within that language. Any language therefore must be understood to have a vocabulary that can be divided into *defined* and *undefined* (or "primitive") words. Since defined words are ultimately defined by means of primitive (undefined) words, the difficulty arises of accounting for the meaning of those primitives. This problem is not ordinarily considered to be one in the philosophy of science, but falls within the domain of cognitive science. The most important modes of definition are **empirical analysis; explication; implicit definition; meaning analysis; nominal definition;** and **ostensive definition.**

Definitions, complete/partial. A definition qualifies as complete only if it specifies conditions in its definiens that are both necessary and sufficient for the application of its definiendum. Definitions that provide only sufficient or only necessary conditions are therefore merely partial. See also **reduction sentences.**

Degrees of belief. A person's measure of credibility (or strength of conviction) that something is the case, where those degrees of belief are usually indexed by means of betting odds. For example, if a person were willing to bet even money at odds of 2 : 1 against Duke repeating as the basketball champion of the NCAA, that would presumably make the person's degree of belief that Duke will win equal to $1/3$ (or 33 percent), and that Duke will lose equal to $2/3$ (or 66 percent). Theories of knowledge that do without acceptance and rejection rules tend to make this a basic concept. See also **acceptance and rejection rules; Bayesianism.**

Demarcation, the problem of. That of establishing a criterion for distinguishing between scientific and non-scientific assertions. Popper especially emphasizes the importance of this problem, which is very different from the logical positivist problem of meaningfulness, which was the problem of establishing a criterion for distinguishing between meaningful and meaningless assertions. Even assertions that are non-scientific might still qualify as meaningful. See also **meaningfulness, the problem of.**

Descartes, René (1596–1650). French mathematician and philosopher, has often been referred to as the father of modern philosophy. This accolade is meant to emphasize his role in shifting attention from the objective (external) world to the subjective (internal) mind. Descartes employed a method now referred to as "Cartesian doubt" to challenge the credibility of everything he believed in order to determine whether there was anything about which he could be certain. Things that he found to be incapable of doubting (or "indubitable") were taken to be true, thereby forging an alliance between psychology and epistemology. Since some persons are more credulous than others, there seems to be no fixed class of indubitable propositions, a problem that might be overcome (at least, in part) by interpreting his position as focusing not on beliefs that actually are beyond all doubt but on those that should be beyond all doubt instead. Some philosophers have questioned the existence of indubitable beliefs on any suitable interpretation. See also **certainty, personal; doubt, Cartesian.**

Descriptive/normative distinction (also known as the is/ought distinction). The difference between the way things are and the way they ought to be. Philosophical inquiries are frequently directed at the discovery of how things should be with respect to understanding the nature of knowledge, truth, science, ethics, art, and other subjects or activities, especially with respect to their conceptual and theoretical frameworks, which makes philosophy a normative activity. But some philosophers embrace alternative conceptions that make philosophy descriptive. See also **explication.**

Determinism/indeterminism. The thesis of *determinism*, strictly speaking, maintains that every event occurs as the only physically possible outcome of its antecedent conditions in conformity with universal laws. The thesis of *indeterminism* maintains that some events that occur are not the only possible outcomes of their antecedent conditions, but instead occur as one among various possible outcomes within a fixed set in accord with probabilistic laws. These theses are both compatible with universal causation, which maintains that every event that occurs has a cause. The thesis of determinism is also incompatible with *noncausation*, which affirms that some events have no causes at all (possibly because they are miraculous), but the thesis of indeterminism by itself does not preclude non-causation. These theses concern properties of the world and should be distinguished from counterparts concerning our beliefs about the properties of the world.

Determinism/noncausation. The thesis of determinism as universal causation is sometimes contrasted with the thesis that at least some events are not caused, where noncausation is equated with indeterminism. Alternatively, indeterminism is viewed not as noncausation but as a special kind of (probabilistic) causation instead. See also **determinism/indeterminism.**

Deterministic law. A deterministic law maintains that every event that satisfies specified conditions has a unique nomically possible outcome. Those conditions must (implicitly or explicitly) include the presence or the absence of every property that makes a difference to that outcome phenomenon. Otherwise, some nomically relevant property is left unspecified and, depending upon its presence or absence in any specific instance, that outcome may or may not occur, contrary to the character of deterministic laws. Deterministic hypotheses thus appear to describe what are taken as complete sets of relevant conditions, which can be subjected to empirical tests that may possibly refute them, in which case alternative deterministic hypotheses may be advanced in their place. But the phenomenon under consideration could turn out to be probabilistic instead of deterministic. The completeness of such laws is sometimes handled by implied **ceteris paribus clauses** or by viewing those laws as subjunctive idealizations.

Deterministic theory. A set of deterministic laws that apply to a common domain. Alternatively, any theory that permits only one physically possible outcome for instances of its laws. See also **determinisitic law.**

Direct inference. Inference from an hypothesis to its consequences (or from a cause to its effects) is sometimes referred to as a matter of *direct* inference, while inference from its consequences to an hypothesis (or from an effect to its cause) is sometimes referred to as *inverse* inference. Other examples may include arguments by analogy, statistical syllogisms, and enumerative inductions as special cases.

Directly evident/self-evident. Property of a proposition that renders it immediately known simply because of the meanings of the terms involved. For example, "The whole is equal to the sum of its parts" and "I was born sometime before yesterday." Alternatively, a property of sentences describing one's mental states, which cannot be other than as they appear to be if introspection, in particular, is completely reliable.

Direct perception. Perception that involves no **inference.** The results of direct perception are sometimes supposed to be incapable of being mistaken, but various phenomena of illusions, delusions, and hallucinations make that a difficult thesis to defend. When direct perception is characterized as involving the use of language to describe the contents of experience, the possibility of misdescription supports the view that even what we call direct perception is fallible. See also **fallibilism; incorrigibility; justification, causal theories of; knowledge, basic; reliabilism.**

Discovery, context of. See **context of discovery/ context of justification.**

Dispositional predicates. Any word, phrase, or expression that refers to a **disposition.** Such predicates often but not always have the form "-ible," "-able," and such, but many common nouns, such as words for colors, shapes, and sizes, also appear to be dispositional in kind. See also **observable/theoretical distinction.**

Dispositions. Tendencies to display specific outcome responses under suitable conditions. Conductivity, malleability, etc., among physical properties, and sincerity, honesty, etc., among psychological properties, are examples, where things that have these properties tend to display various specific kinds of behavior under various specific circumstances. When a distinction is drawn between "observable" and "unobservable" properties, dispositions are sometimes viewed as unobservable properties with observable manifestations, which are not assumed to exhaust their content. Properties classified as "observable" or "theoretical" may also be dispositional. Important work on dispositions has been done by **Nelson Goodman** and by **Karl R. Popper,** among others.

Dispositions, probabilistic. See **probability, propensity interpretation of.**

Doubt. The mental state of uncertainty or of nonbelief; the opposite of believing or of disbelieving. Alternatively, the act of withholding belief or of not knowing what to believe about some matter under consideration.

Doubt, Cartesian. The methodological tactic adopted by Descartes of deliberately withholding assent from any belief that he found himself able to doubt. Thus, he could doubt the existence of the external world because there might be an Evil Genius (or deceiving demon) who is misleading him. Ultimately, the only belief that he found himself incapable of doubting was the belief that he was doubting since, the more he doubted that belief, the more convinced he became of its truth. From the existence of doubts, Descartes inferred his existence as a thing that doubts (or, more broadly, that thinks) and his essence as a doubting (or thinking) thing. Thus, Descartes proposed, "Cogito ergo sum!" ("I think, therefore I am!"). Bertrand Russell has maintained that Descartes was entitled to infer only the existence of doubts and not his existence as a thinking thing. His argument, nevertheless, has been one of the most studied and influential of all in philosophy.

Duhem thesis. (Also known as the Quine-Duhem thesis.) The view that hypotheses, even in science, are never subject to empirical test one by one but only in sets. The results of observations and of experiments, for example, typically depend upon various assumptions other than the truth or falsity of the hypothesis under investigation. These may concern *background knowledge* (that a certain object is called the Moon), *auxiliary hypotheses* (concerning the mode of function of an instrument, such as a telescope, for example), and *initial conditions* (that this telescope is being used to observe the Moon). When Galileo turned his telescope to observe the Moon and reported that its surface was irregular and pockmarked, the bishops of Padua, who accepted the Aristotelian doctrine that heavenly objects are perfectly spherical and smooth, refused to look through the telescope on the grounds that it must be working improperly (that the appearance of objects must be altered when they are observed by telescope, etc.). And, indeed, unless Galileo's background assumptions, auxiliary hypotheses, and initial conditions were as he took them to be, his observations of the Moon would not serve as a suitable test of the Aristotelian doctrine.

E

Empirical adequacy. Any scientific theory that is compatible with the results of observation and experiment may be said to satisfy the condition of empirical adequacy. Alternatively, the empirical content of a scientific theory may be characterized as restricted to its observable consequences, where any theory with the same set of observable consequences possesses the same empirical adequacy. See also **instrumentalism/realism.**

Empirical analysis. An empirical analysis may occur when some examples or samples of the kind of thing under consideration are available for investigation, which can afford an enhanced understanding of things of that kind. Stuff of the kind *gold*, for example, was familiar to ancient peoples, who knew it was a yellowish, malleable metal. But they did not know that atoms of gold have the atomic number 79 as a function of the number of protons in the nucleus of atoms of that kind. This discovery, which did not occur until the nineteenth century, afforded a foundation for redefining the meaning of "gold" by means of that property. Empirical analyses are either true or false insofar as they accurately or inaccurately report the properties of things of the sample/example kind. They are both empirical and fallible. See also **definitions.**

Empirical science. Aims at the discovery of those principles by means of which the singular events and the general phenomena that occur during the course of the world's history might be explained and predicted systematically. These principles, which are usually identified as **laws of nature,** are supposed to be accessible to experience and subject to empirical test on the basis of observation and experimentation. Alternatively, the goal of empirical science can be described as that of constructing models of the world. The models that scientists construct are usually called **theories.**

Empiricism. Any variety of the view that knowledge is derived from experience; hence, that there is no a priori knowledge, if such knowledge is supposed to be innate or inborn or independent of experience. Alternatively, the view that the meaning or the truth of hypotheses about the world depends on the existence or non-existence of specific phenomena that are directly accessible to (or testable by means of) perception. The possibility of analytic knowledge in the form of sentences whose truth or falsity follows from a language alone is not always denied, provided that knowledge of such a language is consistent with empiricist principles. Various versions of empiricism tend to be distinguished by means of whether they affirm or deny the existence of foundations for knowledge in the form of beliefs whose truth or falsity can be reliably established on the basis of experience. These beliefs in turn are supposed to serve as a foundation for the inferential acquisition, deductively or inductively, of other knowledge. Empiricist views that endorse the conception of infallible (or incorrigible) foundations for knowledge contrast with others that deny their existence.

Empiricism, Humean. The version of empiricism according to which every meaningful belief originates in, and is reducible to, ideas that arise from impressions in experience. Hence, if an idea cannot be traced back to impressions in experience that gave rise to it (directly, if that idea is simple, or indirectly, if it is complex), then it is not meaningful and ought to be rejected. Hume employed this principle with devastating effect on, among others, the notions of self, of object, and of causation. Characteristically, he identified three elements of complex ideas: (1) a resemblance relation, (2) a regular proximity in space and time relation, (3) and a necessary connection relation. According to Hume, with respect to the idea of causation in the case of the striking of a match causing the lighting of the match, for example, what we can discern in experience is, first, a relation of resemblance between differerent instances of strikings (of lightings, etc.); and, second, a regular proximity in space and time, such that the instances of strikings occur temporally prior to and within the same spatial locale as instances of lightings; but where, third, no natural necessity (or "mustness") connecting those events can be detected by means of experience. Hume suggested that the strongest conception of causation that could be justified on the basis of his principle was reducible to (1) and (2), while abandoning (3). If there are no necessary connections that relate causes to effects, however, then, as Hume himself emphasized, there seems to be no reason to expect that the future must resemble the past. Hume thereby yielded what has come to be known as the problem of induction, namely: What rational basis do we have for systematically anticipating the course of future events? See also **Hume, David; induction, the problem of.**

Empiricism, principle of. (1) Denies the existence of any synthetic a priori knowledge; (2) asserts that decisions about the acceptance of hypotheses and theories in science must be based upon observation and experimentation. See also **analytic/synthetic distinction; a priori/a posteriori distinction; empiricism; idealism, Kantian; Popper, Karl R.**

Empiricism, radical. A thesis of William James maintaining that the meaningfulness or the truth of our beliefs does not depend upon whether those beliefs

45

originated in suitable sensory experiences but rather whether the sensory experiences that those beliefs predict obtain or would obtain if suitable conditions were realized, in which case we are entitled to treat them as true. While James, like other empiricists, rejects the existence of innate or inborn knowledge, he strongly diverges from Hume by denying that the origins of an idea are the measure of its epistemic significance or value. His position has been influential as a version of pragmatism. See also **empiricism; empiricism, Humean; pragmatism;** and **truth, pragmatic theory of.**

Empiricism/Rationalism. See also **empiricism** and **rationalism.**

Empiricism, the liberal thesis of. The denial of the narrow thesis of empiricism, especially in logical positivism and logical empiricism, mainly because of difficulties encountered in formalizing the meaning of **dispositional predicates.** See also **empiricism, the narrow thesis of; observable/theoretical distinction; reduction sentences.**

Empiricism, the narrow thesis of. Especially in logical positivism and logical empiricism, the contention that every significant non-analytic hypothesis in empirical science either is an observation sentence or is reducible to observation sentences and logical operators. See also **empiricism, the liberal thesis of.**

Entrenchment, degree of. A predicate's record of past use in successful predictions is known as its degree of entrenchment in the theory of projectibility advanced by **Nelson Goodman.** See also **induction, the new problem of; projectible predicates.**

Epistemic circularity. The allegedly vicious circularity involved in maintaining that one must be epistemically justified in believing one's own definition of epistemic justification. See also **paradox of analysis.**

Epistemic resources. The resources available for solving epistemic problems, including one's language, powers of observation, powers of deductive and of inductive inference, and also of imagination and conjecture.

Epistemology (the theory of knowledge). The study of the **conditions of knowledge** and of efforts to resolve the **problem of criteria.**

Epistemology, evolutionary. See also **evolutionary epistemology.**

Epistemology, naturalized. See also **naturalized epistemology.**

Essentialism. The view that everything has an essence that is distinctive of that thing individually or of everything of that kind collectively. Aristotle was the principal proponent of essentialism during the history of philosophy. According to him, the essence of man (what man is) is a rational animal. Among contemporary philosophers, Saul Kripke has stimulated a resurgence of interest in essentialism by elaborating the theses that proper names acquire their meaning by virtue of a causal connection to their referents (that for which they stand) rather than by virtue of descriptions and that predicates and properties may also be similarly related.

Ethics of belief. The doctrine, advanced by William Clifford, that we are only morally entitled to believe what we are logically entitled to believe. Hence, we are never entitled to believe anything that is not appropriately supported by the available relevant evidence. Alternatively, the idea that nothing may be accepted as true simply as an article of faith.

Evidence. That which tends to show that something is

the case. It can take the form of observations or experiments (or of reports of observations or experiments) or of linguistic premises that support deductive or inductive reasoning in relation to some hypothesis. Various arguments provide grounds, reasons, or evidence for conclusions.

Evidentialism. The view that whether or not a person is justified in holding a belief is determined exclusively by the quantity and the quality of the evidence that person has for that belief. Evidentialism is intended as an alternative to **reliabilism** and **causal theories of justification**.

Evidential relevance. A sentence *e* is evidentially relevant to another sentence *h* when the truth or falsity of *e* makes a difference to the truth or falsity of *h*. See also **arguments, deductive; arguments, inductive**.

Evidential support. See arguments; evidence.

Evil demon hypothesis. The hypothesis, first introduced by René Descartes, asserting the possible existence of a powerful and malicious demon whose only purpose is to deceive us into thinking that something is the case when it is not. Indeed, the false beliefs induced in us by such a demon might be ones we are incapable of detecting. According to Descartes, the beliefs about which we might be deceived include our perceptual beliefs, memory beliefs, beliefs about our mental states, and even beliefs about mathematics. Since the evil demon hypothesis is logically possible, if knowledge requires the logical impossibility of being mistaken, then no one can ever know anything about the objects of perception, past events, mental states, or mathematics. Similar considerations support the view that we might be *brains in vats,* where our beliefs are induced by means of artificial neural stimulation. Some philosophers take the hypothesis to demonstrate the impossibility of knowledge, while others interpret it as indicating that, if immunity from mistakes is a condition for knowledge, then the kind of immunity involved must be freedom from certain non-logical possibilities of error rather than from logical possibilities of error.

Evolutionary epistemology. The attempt to develop a theory of knowledge that envisions the growth of knowledge as an evolutionary process. Among the difficulties that this position confronts are (1) overcoming the traditional distinction between epistemology as normative and evolution as descriptive, since presently available or currently utilized methods or procedures may or may not be capable of improvement; (2) accounting for the differences between cultural evolution as Lamarckian (involving the inheritance of acquired characterisitics) and genetic evolution as Darwinian (denying the inheritance of acquired characteristics); and (3) establishing why traditional conceptions of justification as grounds, reasons, or evidence ought to be displaced by evolutionary explanations for why the beliefs we have should be regarded as the beliefs we ought to have. Those who pursue this approach include Donald Campbell and David Hull.

Existential generalization. Any sentence of the form, "Some *As* are *Bs*" or, more generally, any sentence that asserts the existence of at least one thing of any kind.

Expectability, nomic. See also **nomic expectability.**

Explanation. An acceptable answer to an explanation-seeking why-question. At least two kinds of explanation are normally distinguished: (1) *ordinary explanations,* where to explain something to someone tends to be a process of settling their doubts or puzzlement, whether or not by means of answers to questions that are either well-founded or true (as it has been explored in the work of Peter Achinstein, among others); and, (2) *scientific explanations,* where to explain something tends to be a

49

process of showing that the phenomenon of interest occurred in accordance with or by virtue of specific laws of nature and antecedent conditions attending the occurrence of that phenomenon. These are independent concepts, since explanations that are personally satisfying need make no reference to laws, while explanations that make reference to laws need not be psychologically satisfying. Some theoreticians, such as Michael Scriven and Bas van Fraassen, have suggested that even explanations in science do not require reference to natural laws. The most influential philosophers who have dealt with this problem, including **Carl G. Hempel** and **Wesley C. Salmon**, however, have thought otherwise. See also **explanation, scientific.**

Explanation, causal-relevance model of. The realization that statistically relevant properties are not necessarily causally relevant and may therefore be explanatorily irrelevant motivated the search for yet another model of explanation intended to capture the notion that properties are explanatorily relevant only if they are causally (or nomically) relevant. This can be done by adopting the single-case version of the propensity interpretation of probability in lieu of the long-run version of the frequency interpretation. Thus, a specific set of properties may possess a causal tendency to produce (or "bring about") a specific outcome with a certain strength of tendency, which is of maximal (or "universal") strength in the case of deterministic laws and of partial (or "probabilistic") strength in the case of indeterministic laws. According to the model introduced by James H. Fetzer, explanations always assume the form of arguments, no matter whether they are deterministic-deductive or indeterministic-probabilistic in kind, and always specify associated degrees of *nomic expectability*, even though there is no requirement of a relation of high probability between the explanans and the explanandum of a probabilistic explanation. The fundamental desideratum that explanations are intended to satisfy, however, is not that of nomic expectability but rather that of *nomic responsibility*, by displaying the compete set of relevant conditions whose presence made a difference to the occurrence of the explanandum outcome. An alternative version has been elaborated by Peter Railton, which is know as the D-N-P (or "deductive-nomological-probabilistic") model of explanation. Employing the notion of an ideal explanatory text, Railton suggests that a complete scientific explanation of a singular event would require a theoretical explanation of the law that occurs in the explanans, where that law and the description of antecedent conditions, in turn, explains the occurrence of the explanandum outcome. One feature that distinguishes Railton's approach is that he retains the conception of explanations as arguments in the case of explanations involving universal laws, but abandons it in the case of explanations involving probabilistic laws. Other differences that distinguish these views involve questions of semantics with respect to the interpretation of probabilities as propensities.

Explanation, causal vs. non-causal. Explanations that explain by reference to temporally prior initial conditions and causal laws are causal explanations, while others that explain by reference to temporally simultaneous initial conditions and non-causal laws are non-causal explanations.

Explanation, covering-law model of. The most influential theory of explanation has been the covering-law model, which combines the conception of explanation by means of subsumption with the conception that explanations are arguments. The principal desideratum that explanations are supposed to fulfill is that of *nomic expectability,* in the sense that explanations in science display the extent to which the phenomena that they explain were to be expected on the basis of the antecedent conditions that attended that outcome and relevant natural laws. If those laws happen to be laws of universal form, then a description of the event to be explained (known as the *explanandum*) can be deduced from a description of those antecedent conditions and natural laws (known as the *explanans*). If the laws happen to be laws of statistical (or of probabilistic) form, then a description of the event to be explained does not follow from its explanans but instead receives inductive support, where the quantity of support is determined by the strength of the corresponding law. The classic model in which laws of universal form provide the general premises for deducing the explanandum is therefore known as the *deductive-nomological* (or D-N) model of explanation, while the model in which laws of statistical (or of probabilistic) form provide the general premises for inducing the explanandum is known as the *inductive-statistical* (or I-S) model of explanation. The foremost proponent of the covering-law model of explanation has been **Carl G. Hempel**, whose voluminous writings on this subject have been enormously influential. In its early formulations, he also subscribed to *the symmetry thesis,* according to which every adequate scientific explanation could have served as the basis for an adequate scientific prediction, had its explanans been taken into account at a suitable time, and conversely. But in his later work, Hempel tends to separate knowledge of why something is the case from knowledge that something is the case, where knowledge-why provides knowledge-that, but not conversely. This suggests that scientific predictions can qualify as adequate even when they lack any potential explanatory significance. A difficulty with I-S explanations that Hempel was never able to resolve concerns the elaboration of a suitable conception of maximal specificity, which appears to require an intensional conception of nomic probability.

Explanation, philosophical. An explanation that appeals to reasons rather than causes in answering a why-question. Alternatively, an explanation that appeals to at least one premise whose truth or falsity cannot be established on the basis of exclusively scientific methods of inquiry. Examples of explanations in this sense are **explications**, which have the character of recommendations or proposals. The nature of philosophical explanations is controversial, and some philosophers even deny their existence. See also **definitions.**

Explanation, pragmatics of. Any analysis of explanation viewing explanation as a relation involving persons and their beliefs. Studies of the pragmatics of explanation have been advanced by Michael Scriven, Peter Achinstein, and Bas van Fraassen, among others. See also **pragmatics.**

Explanation, probabilistic. See explanation, scientific.

Explanation, scientific. The most widely discussed models of scientific explanation accept the principle that explanation in science involves the subsumption of the phenomenon to be explained as an instance of a natural law. According to some of these accounts, explanations have the form of arguments, while others deny that explanations are arguments. Some assume that the basic desideratum explanations in science have to fulfill is that of nomic expectability, while others emphasize instead statistical relevance or causal relevance. The three principal models of scientific explanation are the covering-law model, the statistical-relevance model, and the causal-relevance model. But other models have been proposed, in particular, in relation to the theory of probabilistic explanation. See also **explanation, causal-relevance model of; explanation, covering-law model of; explanation, probabilistic; explanation, statistical-relevance model of; explanations, aleatory.**

Explanation, statistical-relevance model of. Among the problems that afflicted the covering-law model of explanation was its apparent incapacity to cope with problems of relevance. That John Jones did not become pregnant during the year, for example, could be explained by observing that Jones regularly took his wife's birth control pills during the year together with the covering law that any man who regularly takes his wife's birth control pills during the year does not become pregnant. This argument satisfies Hempel's conditions for D-N explanations, yet seems to be unsatisfactory as an explanation. That Mary Smith recovered from her cold after two weeks could similarly be explained by observing that she took vitamin C in large quantities for two weeks, and that almost everyone who takes vitamin C in large quantities for two weeks recovers from their colds. This argument likewise satisfies Hempel's conditions for I-S explanation. The difficulty is that men do not become pregnant anyway, whether they take birth control pills or not, and that most colds tend to clear up within two weeks anyway, whether you take vitamin C or not. **Wesley C. Salmon** observed that Hempel's conception of explanation was founded upon (what appeared to be) the wrong conception of relevance, since for Hempel a property F is explanatory in relation to an attribute A provided F and A are linked by law, as in the birth control and the cold-recovery cases. He suggested that properties should qualify as explanatorily relevant if and only if they are statistically relevant, where a property F is statistically relevant to an attribute A, in relation to a presupposed reference class R, just in case the probability (frequency) for A in R-and-F differs from the probability (frequency) for A in R. Salmon went further by rejecting the requirement that a relation of high probability must obtain between the explanans and the explanandum of inductive (now "statistical") explanations, on the ground that it rendered the explanation of events that occur only with low probability logically impossible. Taking this same requirement as a necessary condition for an argument to be an acceptable inductive argument, Salmon also rejected the conception of explanations as arguments. Thus, according to the statistical-relevance model of explanation, an explanation involves establishing a set of divisions (or "partitions") to isolate statistically homogeneous subsets, where a singular event is explained by assigning it to the homogeneous partition that represents the complete set of statistically relevant properties antecedent to that singular event. Each such event then possesses an objective probability (frequency) for its occurrence in relation to that complete set of reference conditions, but these values do not occur as degrees of nomic expectability linking explanans and explananum, as they do in Hempel's scheme. By identifying universal laws with probabilities of value one, Salmon proposed that deductive explanations ought to be viewed as a limiting case of statistical explanations, where explanations of neither kind need to be understood as having the form of arguments. Although the statistical-relevance model of explanation initially appeared to hold great promise, it has encountered difficulties that appear to be insurmountable because statistically relevant properties are not necessarily causally relevant properties and may be explanatorily irrelevant, too. See also **explana-**

tion, causal-relevance model of; explanation, covering-law model of.

Explanation, theoretical. Any explanation of a phenomeon involving appeals to any theory. Alternatively, any explanation of a law of nature by appealing to a theory from which a description of that law can be derived.

Explanation vs. justification. An explanation of why something is the case does not establish that it ought to be the case, which is another question. If the thesis of universal causation is true, for example, then every event is explainable, in principle, but that does not show that every event is morally justifiable. See also **descriptive/normative distinction; determinism/indeterminism.**

Explanationism. The thesis that our knowledge of the external world is the product of the best available explanation-providing answers to explanation-seeking-why questions. Alternatively, that our knowledge is always the product of the best available explanation for a phenomenon. See also **explanation; explanation, scientific; inference to the best explanation.**

Explanations, aleatory. Explanations that assume the canonical form, "X because Y despite Z," where "X" describes the explanandum phenomenon, "Y" describes conditions that contributed to its occurrence, and "Z" describes those factors, if any, that inhibited its occurrence. This approach has been advanced by Paul Humphreys as an alternative to the covering-law, statistical-relevance, and causal-relevance models of explanation, but it may be compatible with causal-relevance models, only differing from them pragmatically. See also **explanation, causal-relevance model of.**

Explication. The purpose of an explication is to take a somewhat vague and ambiguous word, phrase, or expression and subject it to critical scrutiny, where the result is a recommendation or proposal as to how it might best be understood in order to achieve certain theoretical or philosophical objectives. Words such as "science," "theory," and "law," for example, might be subject to explication in an attempt to develop a framework for better understanding the nature of science. Since explications have the character of recommendations, they can be qualified as more or less adequate, but they cannot be characterized as either true or false. The methodology of explication affords a solution to one version of the **paradox of analysis**. See also **definitions**.

Externalism. The view that whether a true belief is an item of knowledge, or whether a true belief is appropriately justified to be an item of knowledge, is exclusively a function of whether there is a suitable causal connection between one's belief and the external state of affairs that belief is about. Such a connection is established when the process or mechanism producing that belief is reliable. Under this view, it is not a necessary condition that the subject be aware of that connection, be able to describe that connection, or even be able, under certain conditions, to offer reasons that justify that belief as being the product of a reliable process or mechanism. See also **reliabilism.**

External world. Everything there is the existence of which does not depend upon the existence of any human mind. Alternatively, that which exists and would continue to exist even if there were no human minds. Thus, neither human sensations nor human perceptions are properties of the external world. Phenomenalists may therefore contend that the external world is nothing but a construction from sensations and perceptions. Alternatively, everything there is. Synonymous with the *physical world*. See also **perception; phenomenalism, phenomenalist theory of.**

F

Facts. Sometimes supposed to be that of which the world is made. According to *logical atomism*, for example, the world is composed of facts, not of things. More circumspect conceptions tend to identify facts with *true sentences* (true propositions, true statements). That snow is white is a fact just in case a sentence in some specific language that makes that assertion (or some like proposition or statment) is true. Facts cannot be restricted to space/time, moreover, since that $2 + 2 = 4$ appears to be as much a fact as that snow is white. If facts are true sentences, then any attempt to define truth as the correspondence of a sentence to a fact is an example of circular reasoning. See also **truth, correspondence theory of.**

Fallibilism. The view that we could be mistaken about everything we think we know because it might be false. There are three species of fallibilism. One (traditional) view maintains merely that everything we believe we know is something about which we might be mistaken, thereby retaining the traditional conception of knowledge as warranted, true belief. When our beliefs are not true, we simply do not know that we do not know. The second (Popperian) view, however, rejects the traditional approach in favor of the conception of knowledge as warranted belief, which might be true or not. So the scientific knowledge of the time can be false. A third (pragmatic) view holds that truth remains necessary for knowledge but that truth is a matter of warranted assertability relative to the available evidence, where changes in the available evidence across time can affect changes in truth-value across time. Fallibilism can be restricted to synthetic sentences, while acknowledging that analytic sentences can be known with certainty, depending upon the acceptability of the analytic/synthetic distinction. An important feature of fallibilism of every kind is the denial that knowledge by perception is **incorrigible.**

Falsifiability. Broadly speaking, a sentence is falsifiable when, under suitable conditions, it could be shown to be false (probably false). Strictly speaking, however, a sentence is falsifiable when it is not contradictory but its negation is deducible from a logically consistent, finite set of sentences describing the results of possible observations and experiments. Different classes of sentences can be verified or falsified. For example, existential generalizations are verifiable but not falsifiable, while universal generalizations are falsifiable but not verifiable. Popper has proposed falsifiability as a criterion of demarcation to separate scientific from nonscientific assertions. See also **demarcation, problem of; meaningfulness, problem of; verifiability.**

Falsification. See **verification.**

Feminist philosophy of science. See **philosophy of science, feminist.**

Formal system. A collection of marks of varied shapes and sizes together with specified axioms, formation rules, and transformation rules qualifies as a formal system. The *formation rules* specify how those marks can be combined to create well-formed formulae (or "sentences") of that system, while the *transformation rules* specify what follows from what, that is, which formulae are syntatically derivable from which other formulae in accordance with the rules. The *specific axioms* of a formal system are primitive (or "unproven") assumptions, which are typically adopted with respect to the elements and relations of some abstract domain as its intended interpretation. A formal system is **sound** when every formula ("theorem") that is derivable from the axioms is true with respect to the intended interpretation. If every sentence that is true with respect to the intended interpretation is also derivable as a theorem, the system is **complete.**

Foundationalism. The view that there are basically known propositions that are neither derived nor derivable from other known propositions or beliefs, and that these basically known propositions are foundational or serve as evidence for other beliefs derived from them or demonstrated by appeal to them. Foundationalists can be either modest or classical depending upon whether they regard these foundational beliefs as privileged but not irrefutable on the basis of future experience **(Peirce)** or whether they regard these foundational beliefs as so certain as to be irrefutable by appeal to any future experience **(Aristotle** and **Descartes).**

G

Generalizations. See also **conditionals; existential generalization; laws of nature; universal generalization.**

Gettier problem. See also **counterexamples, Gettier-style.**

Goodman, Nelson (1906–   ). American philosopher, widely known for his work on conditionals, dispositions, and laws. As an advocate of nominalism, he has supported the notion that there is no more to properties than their sets of instances. Perhaps best known for his research on counterfactual conditionals and projectible predicates, he has written on many other subjects, including aesthetics and the structure of appearance. See also **induction, the new problem of; projectible predicates.**

Growth of knowledge. Problem domain explored by **Karl R. Popper, Thomas S. Kuhn, Imre Lakatos,** and others concerning how scientific theories are accepted, rejected, and changed across time.

H

Hallucinations. The apparent perception of sights, sounds, etc., that do not exist. Alternatively, the sights, sounds, etc., that are mistakenly supposed to exist. See also **illusion, argument from; illusions.**

Hempel, Carl G. (1905–   ). German-American professor at Princeton and Pittsburgh and one of the most influential philosophers of science of the twentieth century. Most widely noted for his work on the nature of explanation, Hempel emphasizes the importance of formal methods utilizing extensional logic in resolving philosophical problems. His articles on confirmation, cognitive significance, and explanation and prediction in both the natural and the social sciences virtually defined these problems for future generations. See also **confirmation, paradoxes of; explanation, covering-law model of.**

High probability, requirement of. (1) In relation to probabilistic conceptions of inductive arguments, where the premises confer a certain probability p upon a conclusion, the high probability requirement makes a conclusion acceptable only if it has a probability greater than 0.5 (sometimes a higher value) and is unacceptable if it has a probability less than 0.5. When it has a probability equal to 0.5, it may be accepted or rejected. (2) In relation to Hempel's inductive-statistical (or I-S) model of explanation, an explanation is not adequate unless its explanans confers a probability equal to or greater than 0.5 upon its explanandum, where this "probability" may be viewed as a measure of evidential support (Hempel's earlier theory) or as a degree of nomic expectability (Hempel's later theory). See also **arguments, inductive; explanation, covering-law model of.**

Historical possibility/necessity/impossibility. A sentence S in a language L describes an historically possible (necessary, impossible) state of affairs or "world" (relative to time t) in relation to L, the set of lawlike sentences N that is true of the world, and the set of historical descriptions true of the world prior to time t if and only if it is not the case that not-S follows from L-and-N-and-H (it is the case that S follows from L-and-N-and-H, but not from L-and-N alone, it is the case that not-S follows from L-and-N-and-H, but not from L-and-N alone). In relation to ordinary English, Newton's laws, and the history of the world until now, it is an historical possibility that the book on my desk will remain at rest until tomorrow (it is an historical necessity that the book on my desk will remain at rest until tomorrow unless it is acted upon by an external force; and it is an historical impossibility that the book on my desk will be acted upon by an external force and nevertheless remain at rest until tomorrow).

History of science. Attempts to reconstruct the hypotheses and theories that different scientists have advanced and the kinds of observations and experiments that they have conducted in their efforts to discover the general principles by means of which the world itself might be understood. Alternatively, the goal of the history of science is to record past efforts to construct models of the world, as that is pursued within empirical science. Some philosophers emphasize the history of science in their study of science as a process, while others analyze the products produced by science. See also **naturalized epistemology; philosophy of science.**

History of science, external. Study of the actual course of events in the growth of knowledge, independently of consideration for how the phenomena should best be understood from a theoretical/normative point of view.

History of science, internal. Reconstruction of the course of events in the growth of knowledge in an attempt to explain what went right and what went wrong from a theoretical/normative point of view.

Holism. The view that individual hypotheses cannot be confirmed or disconfirmed on their own but depend upon the truth or falsity of various other hypotheses that assume the character of theories. Hence, the idea that whole theories rather than specific sentences are the smallest testable units of empirical science. Alternatively, the view that any belief whatsoever can be rationally acceptable, even in the face of seemingly disconfirming evidence, if drastic enough changes in other beliefs are permitted. See also **coherence; fallibilism; truth, coherence theory of; Quine, W. V. O.**

Hume, David (1711–1776). Scottish philosopher, known for critiques of such notions as causation, object, and self, and for his denial of the existence of natural (or non-logical) necessities. According to Hume, any idea that cannot be traced back directly or indirectly to impressions in experience that gave rise to it should be rejected. He denied that causes have to bring about their effects, insisting that the notion of causation was reducible to relations of resemblance and of regular association and emphasized that, since we have no rational warrant to believe in the existence of natural necessities, we have no reason to believe that the future will resemble the past, a difficulty now known as the *problem of induction*. See also **empiricism, Humean; fallibilism, induction, the problem of.**

Hume worlds. Alleged to be worlds (or descriptions of worlds) that have the same histories yet differ with respect to their laws. A special case is that of two worlds with the same histories, where one has laws but the other does not. Strictly speaking, they are logically impossible if laws are nothing more than historical regularities, as in the case of Humean empiricism. They are possible on accounts where laws are more than regularities. See also **empiricism, Humean; laws of nature, regularity theory of.**

Hypothesis. Any conjecture or speculation about how things are, especially in the form of a lawlike sentence or of a scientific theory. Alternatively, any opinion or attitude on any matter where the truth is unknown.

Hypothesis testing, orthodox theory of. A widely followed set of acceptance and rejection principles for statistical hypotheses developed in the work of R. A. Fisher, Jerzy Neyman, and Egon Pearson. Its most important philosophical proponents include Ronald N. Giere and Deborah Mayo.

Hypothetical entities. Any entity described by means of non-observable predicates. Alternatively, anything that cannot be directly observed.

I

Idealism, classic. A position that denies one or more of the tenets of classic realism by asserting, for example, that the nature or existence of the world is logically or causally dependent on the existence of some mind, which might be human or the mind of God. See also **realism, classic.**

Idealism, Kantian. Holds that, even though there is a world whose nature and existence is neither logically nor causally dependent upon the existence of any human mind, the properties of that world are knowable not as they exist apart from experience but only as they are experienced. Although rational beliefs and scientific knowledge may be epistemically virtuous, no methods of inquiry have the capacity to reveal the world as it exists in itself. As such, this position accepts the first tenet of classic realism (except for the possibility of an unknowable God who has created the world), while it denies the second and the third. See also **realism, classic.**

Illusion, argument from. Any argument that appeals to **illusions** in support of the conclusion that perception cannot always be relied upon as a source of knowledge. In its strongest version, the conclusion drawn is that perception can never be relied upon as a source of knowledge, but weaker versions insist instead that we can never be certain that we have not been misled in any specific case. Sometimes appeals are also made to the occurrence of **hallucinations** in support of the contention that what is accessible to us in experience must be either sense data or appearances, insofar as the existence of illusions and hallucinations establishes that we do not have direct access to the properties of objects in the external world.

Illusions. Errors that arise from faulty perceptions or misinterpretations of experience, as when parallel lines appear to converge, dreams are mistaken for reality, and mirages induce false beliefs. Illusions are often said to differ from **hallucinations**, where *hallucinations* involve beliefs in the existence of things that do not exist, while *illusions* involve beliefs in non-existent properties of things that do exist, where other properties of those things may causally contribute to the occurrence of any illusion.

Implicit definition. An implicit definition occurs when a word, phrase, or expression is used within a specific theoretical context, where, even though no meaning is directly assigned to that word, phrase, or expression, it assumes meaning indirectly through its inferential relations to other words, and so forth. Thus, although Newton declined to define the meaning of "gravity," that did not render the word meaningless, since it implicitly acquired its meaning through its occurrence in Newton's laws.

Incommensurability. Relationship between two theories or "paradigms" when one cannot be understood in terms of the other. Especially important in the work of **Thomas S. Kuhn** on the growth of knowledge.

Incorrigibility. Characterizes sentences that report the contents of sense experience when they are supposed to be immune from error. An incorrigible sentence is one that could not possibly be false, not as a matter of logic, but as a matter of epistemic standing. Foundational theories of knowledge may assume the existence of such sentences as their basis.

Indeterminacy of translation. See also **translation, indeterminacy of.**

Indeterminism/determinism. See also **determinism/indeterminism.**

Induction. See also **arguments, inductive.**

Induction by enumeration, the principle of. A rule of this form: if m/n observed As have been Bs, then infer (inductively) that m/n As are Bs, provided that a suitable number of As have been observed under a suitable variety of conditions. Because the inference depends upon observing a sample within a population, it appears to be restricted in application to properties that are observable. Moreover, it may or may not be sufficient to warrant inferences to laws. See also **inference to the best explanation; observable/theoretical distinction.**

Induction, the new problem of. The difficulty, discovered by **Nelson Goodman,** of selecting an appropriate language for the formulation of hypotheses. Consider, for example, the color of emeralds, which might all have been green in the past. By introducing a new color term, "grue," for example, meaning observed prior to time t and green but otherwise blue, any evidence that confirms the hypothesis that all emeralds are green also appears to confirm the hypothesis that all emeralds are grue. So what should we predict about the color of emeralds after time t? This appears to be a linguistic version of the problem of induction, whose solution may depend on identifying the characteristics of projectible predicates. See also **induction, the problem of; projectable predicates.**

Induction, the problem of. The problem of establishing a rational warrant for the belief that the future will resemble the past. As Russell observed, such a relation cannot be established by postulation, since it is false that the future will resemble the past in every respect, and trivial that the future will resemble the past in some respect. The problem appears to require a theory of the nature of laws that goes beyond what Hume, especially, would allow. Among the most promising attempts to deal with this problem has been a pragmatic vindication advanced by **Reichenbach.** See also **empiricism, Humean; Reichenbach, Hans vindication, pragmatic.**

Inductive logic. A set of principles of inductive inference that satisfies the axioms of the calculus of probability. Alternatively, any theory of inductive inference, even when its principles are other than probabilistic.

Inductivism. The view that scientific inquiries can only be successfully conducted by relying upon inductive principles of reasoning, especially the principle of induction by enumeration. The inductivist model of science characterizes it as a process of observation, classification, generalization, and prediction. This view is frequently associated with the work of **Hans Reichenbach** and **Wesley C. Salmon,** who combine the frequency interpretation of probability with a pragmatic vindication of induction by appealing to the principle of induction by enumeration. Alternatively, the advocacy of inductive methods to the exclusion of other methods within any domain of inquiry. See also **arguments, deductive; arguments, inductive; induction by enumeration, the principle of; Reichenbach, Hans; Salmon, Wesley C.; vindication, pragmatic.**

Inference. The psychological process of drawing one thought from another, especially when that process could be justified on the basis of logic. Thus, the free association of ideas does not properly qualify as inference. Alternatively, the logical process of drawing a conclusion from premises. Rules of deduction and induction are called *rules of inference.*

Inference to the best explanation. See also **abduction/abductive inference; abductivism.**

Innate knowledge. See also **knowledge, innate.**

Insight. A capacity or ability to rapidly understand a problem in its full dimensions. Alternatively, the product of the exercise of this ability or capacity. The existence of such a faculty is disputed. See also **intuition.**

Instrumentalism/neo-instrumentalism. Any position viewing theories as instruments for prediction that possess no explanatory significance. Neo-instrumentalism accepts the empirical content of theories as though it exhausted the content of a theory. The defense of such positions may depend upon the tenability of the observable/theoretical distinction. See also **empirical adequacy; realism; theories, underdetermination of.**

Internalism. The view that whatever it is that justifies a person's having a certain belief can be ascertained by the believer on the basis of introspection and that being justified in having a belief requires that the person be aware of what it is that justifies such a belief. While some internalists require only that a believer possess such an awareness of that justification, others insist that, under suitable conditions, a believer must be able to specify the reasons that justify such a belief. See also **reliabilism.**

Interpersonalism. Any theory of epistemic justification asserting that it is at least sometimes necessary for a person to be justified in her belief that she should be able to state, show, or provide to other persons the persuasive reasons that justify her belief.

Intrapersonalism. Any theory of epistemic justification asserting that it is never a necessary condition for a person to be justified in her belief that she should be able to state, show, or provide to other persons the persuasive reasons that justify her belief.

Introspection. A faculty or capacity for deriving knowledge, especially about one's own mental states, by internal observation. Two kinds of knowledge by introspection can be distinguished, those that attend to mental states at the time of their occurrence and those that attend to mental states that have been acquired in the past. When past mental states are the object of contemplation through a process of recollection or remembering, the introspective faculty is also known as that of **memory.**

Intuition. A faculty or capacity for producing intuitive knowledge. In its weak sense, intuition may be merely unconscious inference, which could, under suitable conditions, be characterized deductively or inductively. In its strong sense, intuition is a direct or noninferential capacity.

Intuitive knowledge. Consists of knowledge that is neither directly based on sense experience nor the product of conscious deductive or inductive inference from premises based on sense experience. Alternatively, any form of knowledge that is inborn, innate, or genetic in its origins.

Inverse inference. See also **direct inference.**

J

James, William (1842–1910). American philosopher and psychologist, James (along with **Charles S. Peirce** and **John Dewey**) was one of the founders of **pragmatism.** He also contributed a serious study of psychology, which emphasizes the nature of consciousness. James is famous for formulating the doctrine of **radical empiricism** and for the principle that when the evidence for or against an hypothesis is not sufficient for its acceptance or rejection, we are entitled to believe what we want to believe if accepting such a belief is likely to produce something of moral value that would otherwise not occur. James favored the view that truth is a species of the good and that the moral consequences of a belief can count as relevant evidence for or against it.

Justification, as reason giving. See **internalism.**

Justification, as reason having. See **externalism; justification, causal theories of; reliabilism.**

Justification, causal theories of. Theories of justification that assert that the justification of beliefs is a function of how those beliefs are brought about by relating their specific contents to their causal origins. See also **justification, reliability theories of.**

Justification, coherence theories of. Assert that the justification of an individual's beliefs is a function of the extent to which those beliefs are logically consistent and non-logically coherent with a person's other beliefs instead of being a function of their causal origin or of the reasons given for them.

Justification, context of. See also **context of discovery/context of justification.**

Justification, epistemic vs. moral. Distinguishes between the justification of beliefs (epistemic justification) and the justification of actions (moral justification). See also **acceptance and rejection rules; action, rational; actions; belief; belief, rational.**

Justification, holistic theories of. Assert that the justification of a belief is a function of justification of the corporate structure of one's beliefs in their entirety. Alternatively, the view that any sentence may be held to be true, come what may, provided that one is willing to make appropriate adjustments in one's other beliefs. See also **justification, coherence theories of; truth, coherence theory of.**

Justification, inferential. Any justification that depends upon a suitable deductive or inductive inference from premises that themselves require justification. See also **arguments, deductive; arguments, inductive; knowledge, basic; knowledge, non-basic.**

Justification, non-inferential. Any justification that is not based on suitable deductive or inductive inferences from premises that themselves require justification. Hence, any self-justifying process or procedure, such as direct intuition or sense perception. While non-inferential justifications are sometimes required to be incorrigible, contemporary foundationalists emphasize that sense perception may serve as a non-inferential source of justification, even though its results are not incorrigible. See also **direct perception; incorrigibility; intuition; reliabilism.**

Justification, pragmatic theories of. See also **pragmatism.**

Justification, reliability theories of. The view that the justification of a belief is a function of whether that belief is the product of a reliable belief-producing mechanism, method, or process. Such mechanisms, methods, and processes, however, may not always function reliably under various conditions. Adherents to reliability theories differ over whether the satisfaction of this condition is necessary, sufficient, or both necessary and sufficient for the justification of a belief. See also **reliabilism.**

Justification, theory of. Seeks to define the conditions relative to which it would be appropriate to assert that a specific belief is "justified," "adequately justified," or "completely justified." Ideally, such a theory provides the means that are required to ascertain which beliefs do and do not stand in need of justification, what kind and how much evidence those beliefs must have in order to be justified, and related questions.

Justification, verific. The view that a justification is sufficient or adequate for knowledge only if the justification under consideration entails the truth of the proposition for which it serves as a justification. Alternatively, the view that a person cannot be completely justified in believing a false proposition.

Justification vs. truth. A person may be justified in believing that *p* is true, even when *p* is false; and *p* may be true, even though no one is justified in believing that *p* is true. These are traditionally viewed as independent concepts. There are contemporary theories that tend to identify them, however, especially those that appeal to **coherence theories of truth** as opposed to **coherence theories of justification.** See also **confirmation vs. truth.**

Justifying reasons. Any grounds, reasons, or evidence advanced to justify the acceptance of a belief or the adoption of a decision. Alternatively, a reason that would warrant a person's acceptance of a belief or adoption of a decision were they to accept it as a reason. Alternatively, the faculty of having or of being able to provide justifying reasons.

K

Kant, Immanuel (1724–1804). German philosopher, enormously influential for his work in epistemology and in moral theory. Kant said that he had been awakened from his slumber by the work of **David Hume** who, as an aspect of his critique of causation, denied the existence of necessary connections relating future events to past events. Kant held that these connections were not properties of nature but rather of our experience of nature, because the human mind imposes certain forms and categories (known as *Forms of Intuition* and as *Categories of Understanding*) upon everything that is experienced. Thus, with respect to knowledge of nature, though we cannot know what we are going to experience prior to having an experience, we can know, prior to having an experience, that, whatever we experience, we will experience it as located in Euclidean space and Newtonian time and understand it in terms of the categories of substance and causation. While we can have no knowledge of the-world-as-it-exists-apart-from-experience (the *noumenal* world), we can have knowledge of the-world-as-it-exists-in-experience (the *phenomenal* world), some of which is known a priori. See also **a priori/a posteriori distinction; empiricsm; empiricism, Humean; idealism, Kantian; rationalism.**

Knowing that vs. knowing how (also referred to as propositional vs. non-propositional knowledge.) The difference between two kinds of knowledge, namely: *knowing that* something is the case (such as that Ronald Reagan was twice elected president) and *knowing how* to do something (such as count to five hundred, ride a bicycle, or play chess). Some philosophers hold that knowing that is reducible to knowing how (as in knowing how to answer various kinds of questions, knowing how to perform various kinds of tasks, etc.), while denying that knowing how is reducible to knowing that, but this is a disputed issue. See also **knowing who.**

Knowing who. A kind of non-propositional knowledge that does not appear to be reducible to knowing how, namely: *knowing a person.* Thus, knowing the President of the United States might not be a case of knowing that or of knowing how; especially, knowing the president in this sense is different than knowing who the president is. Since knowing someone in this sense involves *personal acquaintance*, which might be viewed as the possession of knowledge about how that person tends to act under different conditions, how to act toward that person to achieve certain effects, etc., knowing who could still be reducible to a species of knowing how.

Knowing why. A kind of propositional knowledge that explains the reason something is the case, usually but not always by citing its causes. The conditions that have to be satisfied to possess knowledge of this kind are aspects of the theory of **explanation**. See also **explanation, scientific.**

Knowledge. In its *traditional* sense, knowledge is justified, true belief. This conception of knowledge, however, is widely assumed to have been undermined by Gettier-style counterexamples. This makes the explication of an adequate conception of knowledge the major task facing contemporary epistemology. Alternatives include foundationalism, coherentism, internalism, and externalism. In its *scientific* sense, knowledge appears to consist of beliefs that are justified because they have been established by scientific inquiries, even though they may be superseded by later scientific knowledge. Classical Newtonian mechanics, for example, remains the best scientific knowledge of its time, in spite of Einstein's discovery that it appears to be false. The principal task of the philosophy of science seems to be the explication of an adequate conception of scientific method, where **inductivism, deductivism, Bayesianism**, and **abductivism** are among the most important alternatives. See also **epistemology; counterexamples, Gettier-style; philosophy of science.**

Knowledge, an examiner's view of. A person knows that *p* only when her belief that *p* is the case can be supported deductively, inductively, or whatever, not as something that has been done but as something that could be done were it required. (This conception was introduced by Ian Hacking.)

Knowledge, basic (non-demonstrative knowledge, or non-inferential knowledge, or immediate knowledge.) Any knowledge that is not the product of suitable deductive or inductive inferences from other propositions that serve as evidence. Alternatively, knowledge not based upon or derived from other knowledge. Some candidates for basic knowledge include knowledge by sense experience (or by direct perception) and by intuition. Basic knowledge may be viewed as certain and beyond all possibility of empirical refutation (**Aristotle** and Norman Malcolm), but can also be viewed as subject to empirical refutation on the basis of future experience (**Goodman** and **Peirce**). See also **direct perception; foundationalism.**

Knowledge by acquaintance vs. knowledge by description. A distinction drawn by **Bertrand Russell** that is intended to reflect a difference between different ways of knowing something. Knowledge by acquaintance occurs when a person acquires knowledge by virtue of a causal connection between that person and other things (such as other persons, objects, and locations). Knowledge by description occurs when a person learns about other things (such as other persons, objects, and locations), not by personally encountering them, but by encountering descriptions (photographs, paintings, or verbal depictions, for example) of them. Knowledge by description may typically depend upon other knowledge by acquaintance. See also **definite descriptions; knowing who; Russell, Bertrand.**

Knowledge, causal theories of. Theories of knowledge that require a suitable causal connection between a belief and the conditions whose existence make that belief true as a necessary condition for that belief to qualify as an item of knowledge.

Knowledge, classic definition of. The definition of "knowledge" as true belief supported by evidence. Beginning with Plato's *Theateatus*, "knowledge" is viewed as true belief *plus* something that has the function of preventing knowledge from being merely a matter of accident or hunch, superstition or a lucky guess. This conception assumes that knowledge requires satisfying a suitable condition of *evidential justification* that goes beyond having a belief that happens to be true. Included among the varied terms that are employed to characterize this requirement are the following: "warranted," "completely warranted," "justified," "adequately justified," "completely justified," "evident," "self-evident," "warrantedly assertible," "evidence giving the right to be sure," and "reliably produced." Contemporary theories of knowledge, such as **foundationalism, coherentism, internalism**, and **reliabilism**, are distinguished primarily by their respective accounts of the nature of evidential justification. See also **knowledge.**

Knowledge, empirical. Knowledge about the external world, especially knowledge that is justified on the basis of direct perception or inductive or deductive inferences based upon direct perception. Alternatively, any knowledge that is **synthetic** rather than **analytic** and **a posteriori** rather than **a priori**. A distinction may be drawn between empirical and scientific knowledge, where the objects of *empirical knowledge* are singular sentences that describe the contents of relatively isolated regions of space/time and the objects of *scientific knowledge* are generalizations (hypotheses and theories) about laws of nature that define the world's structure. Scientific knowledge can then be said to be based on empirical knowledge, yet not be reducible to it. Such a distinction may be more misleading than illuminating, however, since scientific inquiry includes the study of specific instances of black holes, orbiting planets, and other particular phenomena. See also **empirical adequacy; instrumentalism/neo-instrumentalism; knowledge, scientific; observable/theoretical distinction.**

Knowledge, growth of. See also **growth of knowledge.**

Knowledge, innate. Knowledge that one is said to have just in case it (1) could not be the product of either deductive or inductive inference from other knowledge, (2) could not possibly have been acquired by reliance upon beliefs that are directly or indirectly based upon observations or perceptions during a person's lifetime, and (3) has not been induced by divine illumination (God's instruction) during that person's lifetime. Alternatively, knowledge that is genetic or instinctual in character, which one is born with and does not acquire by reasoning or by perception. Whether introspection can be viewed as a source of innate knowledge is debatable.

Knowledge, non-basic (as opposed to basic knowledge, immediate knowledge, or non-inferential knowledge). Characterizes true or at least warranted beliefs that are capable of being adequately justified on the basis of other beliefs, as in the case of conclusions that are supported by inductive or by deductive arguments, which serve as evidence for those beliefs. Alternatively, knowledge based upon, or capable of being inferred from, other propositions that are known but not justified by appeal to other known propositions. Classically defined in terms of warranted, true belief. See also **fallibilism; knowledge, basic; knowledge, innate.**

Knowledge, paranormal. Characterizes knowledge

that is alleged to exist but that is neither innate nor directly or indirectly the product of inductive or deductive inferences from other knowledge that is directly or indirectly based upon sense experience. Alternatively, knowledge based upon extrasensory perception (ESP), sometimes associated with *telepathy* (or direct knowledge of the contents of another person's mind); *precognition* (or non-inferential knowledge about the course of future events); *retrocognition* (or non-inferential knowledge about the course of past events); and *clairvoyance* (or knowledge of present but distant events without the benefit of any causal relation thereto, such as by telephone, television, etc.). The existence of knowledge of their kinds is denied by most theories of knowledge and remains in dispute.

Knowledge, perfect vs. imperfect. A distinction introduced by Rudolf Carnap to capture the difference between warranted beliefs that could not possibly be affected by any future experience and warranted beliefs that could possibly be affected by future experience. In Carnap's view, empirical (or scientific) knowledge is always imperfect, while only a priori (or analytic) knowledge can ever qualify as perfect.

Knowledge, pragmatic theories of. See **pragmatism.**

Knowledge, private. Knowledge that a person is said to have just in case that knowledge is caused by conditions that are transitory, ephemeral, and open only to that person for a limited interval of time. Alternatively, knowledge based upon evidence that is accessible only to that person, which cannot be repeated by others. Some epistemologists deny that private knowledge properly qualifies as "knowledge."

Knowledge, propositional. See also **knowing that vs. knowing how.**

Knowledge, reliability theories of. Any theory that maintains that whether a true belief qualifies as an item of knowledge depends on whether it has been produced by a reliable belief-producing method, mechanism, or process. Under such a view, justification, construed as a reason-giving activity, is not necessary for knowledge. Advocates of this approach often hold that reliability is both necessary and sufficient for a true belief to qualify as an item of knowledge. See also **reliabilism.**

Knowledge, scientific. Knowledge that results from the application of scientific methods of inquiry. Typically, scientific knowledge is general knowledge of empirical regularities or of laws of nature, which is formalized by means of scientific theories. The most important philosophical explications of scientific methods are **inductivism, Bayesianism, deductivism,** and **abductivism,** but the alternatives include **orthodox statistical hypothesis testing.** When the **observable/theoretical distinction** is embraced, crucial differences emerge that differentiate realists from instrumentalists and neo-instrumentalists. See also **empirical knowledge; instrumentalism/ neo-instrumentalism; laws of nature; realism; realism, scientific; theories, scientific.**

Knowledge, strong (knowing strongly). A true belief that is completely justified, or justifiable, by evidence that guarantees the logical certainty of that belief rather than the non-logical certainty of that belief. Alternatively, a completely justified true belief not subject to rejection on the basis of future experience; deductive knowledge based on logically certain premises; infallible knowledge.

Knowledge, weak (knowing weakly). A true belief that is not completely justified, or justifiable, by evidence that guarantees the logical or non-logical certainty of the belief. Alternatively, any completely justified true belief subject to rejection on the basis of future experience; any inductive knowledge based upon evidence that is not logically certain; fallible knowledge; empirical knowledge.

Kuhn, Thomas S. (1922–   ). An American historian and philosopher of science affiliated with MIT. Kuhn is noted for his work on the nature of scientific revolutions, in which one dominating theory or "paradigm" is exchanged for another. Enormously influential, his views are frequently contrasted with those of **Karl Popper,** especially because, in Kuhn's view, Poper's conception of science as **conjectures and refutations** may be typical of *revolutionary science* but is not typical of *normal science,* where theories are being nurtured in an effort to eradicate any **anomalies** they confront. See also **incommensurability.**

L

Lakatos, Imre (1922–1974). Hungarian born scholar who joined the London School of Economics and advanced his conception of research programs as the basic unit of the growth of knowledge. Lakatos introduced the distinction between **external** and **internal history of science** and urged that the history of science, properly understood, must be **normative.** See also **research programs.**

Language. A system of signs used for communication between human beings. *Ordinary* languages include English, French, German, and any other used by a community of humans. *Artificial* languages can be constructed for special purposes, such as the development of formal systems, the programming of computers, and the like. See also **pragmatics; semantics; syntax.**

Lawlike sentences. Any sentence that would be a law if it were true. On the approach that has been pursued by Rudolf Carnap, **Nelson Goodman,** and **Carl G. Hempel,** especially, a sentence S in a language L qualifies as a law in L if and only if S is lawlike and S is true in L. The problem is then reduced to discovering those conditions required for S to be lawlike in L. For S to be lawlike, it must not be logically equivalent to any finite conjunction of singular sentences and must have the capacity to support subjunctive conditionals in L, even though S is not true on syntactical or semantical grounds alone. Hempel has proposed that lawlike sentences are formulated by means of "purely qualitative" predicates, whose meanings do not depend on making reference to any specific individual things or to any specific space/time locations. Thus, "Gold is malleable" appears to be a candidate for a lawlike sentence, but "This first piece of jewelry is gold and sells for more than \$500, but the piece just above it is silver and sells for less than \$500" does not. Alternatively, lawlike sentences are sentences that describe laws when they are true. The development of an adequate explication of natural law has proven difficult. See also **laws; laws of nature; projectible predicates.**

Law of likelihood, Hacking's. Proposed by Ian Hacking as a measure of evidential support, asserts (1) that evidence e supports hypothesis $h1$ better than hypothesis $h2$ when the likelihood of $h1$, given e, exceeds that of $h2$, given e; and (2) that evidence e supports $h1$ better than it supports $h2$ when the likelihood ratio of $h1$ to $h2$ exceeds 1. The most promising theories of confirmation seem to be those that are based upon **Bayes's theo-**

rem, upon **likelihoods,** or upon **orthodox statistical hypothesis testing.**

Laws. General principles of behavior to which conformity should be expected. They are often divided into **laws of nature** and **laws of society,** although there are other senses (such as laws of logic, laws of thought, and the like). This distinction can be drawn on the basis of several criteria, because laws of society are created, can be changed, and require enforcement, while laws of nature are discovered, cannot be changed, and cannot be violated. Laws of society are merely conventional, while laws of nature are not. Severe difficulties have been encountered in developing an adequate theory of **laws of nature.**

Laws of nature. The general principles by means of which singular events and general phenomena that occur during the course of the world's history might be explained and predicted systematically. Laws of nature are envisioned as properties of nature independently of our knowledge or belief, while differing from accidental generalizations, on the one hand, and from laws of society, on the other. A central problem, perhaps even *the* central problem, of the philosophy of science, there are several alternative theories of the nature of laws of nature, including the **necessitarian theory,** the **permanent property theory,** the **regularity theory,** and the **unification theory.**

Laws of nature, necessitarian theory of. Maintains that laws involve irreducible theoretical relations between universals. In the case of universal laws, this relation is said to be one of necessitation and, in the case of probabilistic laws, one of probabilification. One or another version of this theory has been endorsed by David Armstrong, by Fred Dretske, and by Michael Tooley. The principal problem confronting this approach is to provide an analysis of the *irreducible theoretical relation* that supplies the basis for distinguishing accidental generalizations from genuine laws. See also **properties; universals.**

Laws of nature, regularity theory of. Maintains that laws are nothing more than uniform regularities that obtain during the course of the world's history. This conception envisions constant conjunctions of properties or events as universal laws and relative or limiting frequencies as statistical laws. It is intended to be entirely compatible with the kind of empiricism reflected by the work of David Hume, whose critique of causation implies that necessary connections cannot be properly viewed as rationally acceptable in an empiricist theory of natural laws. The difficult problem for the regularity theory is to provide criteria for distinguishing correlations from causation and accidental regularities from genuine laws. Among those who endorse the regular theory of laws are **Carl G. Hempel** and **Wesley C. Salmon.** See also **empiricism, Humean.**

Laws of nature, permanent property theory of. Holds that a basic distinction should be drawn between "permanent" and "transient" properties, where permanent properties are contingent dispositions that something cannot lose without also losing a corresponding reference property. Dispositions are viewed, in turn, as single-case causal tendencies of universal or of probabilistic strength. These conceptions provide an ontological foundation for fixing the truth conditions for synthetic subjunctive conditionals. Lawlike sentences are true only when they are maximally specific and are empirically testable by attempts to establish that they are false. This theory has been elaborated in the work of James H. Fetzer. See also **explanation, causal-relevance theory of; probability, propensity interpretation of.**

Laws of nature, unification theory of. Maintains that natural laws are the fewest general propositions from which every natural regularity might be deduced. This view, which originated with F. P. Ramsey, has been developed by David Lewis. A deductive systematization of this kind, however, confronts several difficulties, precisely because mere uniformities are not invariably reflections of lawful necessity. Consequently, Lewis's codifications, even were they successful, could not be guaranteed to separate mere correlations from laws. See also **laws; laws of nature.**

Laws of society. The constitutions, statutes, and regulations governing a city, state, or nation. In American government, they are passed by a legislature, interpreted by a judiciary, and enforced by an executive. They differ from **laws of nature** insofar as laws of society are normative (or concern how things should be) while laws of nature are descriptive (or concern how things are). Laws of society can be violated, require enforcement, and can be changed.

Likelihoods. Functions of conditional probabilities. When the conditional probability for B, given A, equals p, then the likelihood of A, on the assumption that B is true, equals p. When likelihoods are interpreted as a species of logical probability, Hacking's **law of likelihood** can be employed to measure comparative empirical support for hypotheses on the basis of given evidence. Though the values of likelihoods are determined by those of corresponding probabilities, they are not mathematical probabilities and do not satisfy principles of addition, summation, and so forth.

Logic. The study of arguments, which are usually separated into the categories of deductive and inductive. The first system of logic was that of **classical term logic,**

formalized by **Aristotle,** which studied the validity of arguments that can be formulated by means of a restricted class of sentences having specific kinds of logical form. Classical term logic characterizes the conclusions that follow from one premise (called immediate inference) and the conclusions that follow from two premises (called syllogistic inference), when premises and conclusions are restricted to so-called categorical sentences. Until around the mid-nineteenth century, Aristotelian logic was widely viewed as exhaustive of the subject. But the introduction of the **sentential function** by Gottlob Frege revolutionized the subject, and today Aristotelian logic is recognized to be only a special and relatively modest fragment of modern logic, which includes **sentential logic** (or the study of arguments when whole sentences are the basic units of analysis) and **predicate logic** (or the study of arguments when sentences are analyzed on the basis of their internal structure). Although elementary logic is exclusively extensional (or "truth functional"), advanced logic pursues the formalization of intensional relations that are not merely truth-functional, including the nature of subjunctive, causal, and probabilistic conditionals, but also set theory, recursive function theory, and the theory of models. See also **arguments; arguments, deductive; arguments, inductive; logic, extensional; logic, intensional.**

Logic, classical term. A system of logic studied by Aristotle that is restricted to the validity of arguments that are composed of sentences of four basic forms called "categorical sentences," namely: (A) *universal affirmative*: All S are P; (E) *universal negative*: No S are P; (I) *particular affirmative*: Some S are P; and (O) *particular negative*: Some S are non-P. There are two principal branches, know as *immediate inference* (which studies arguments having one categorical premise and one categorical conclusion) and *syllogistic inference* (which studies arguments having two categorical premises and one categorical conclusion). Medieval logicians discovered that two sets of logical relations are involved here, depending upon whether the subject (*S*-term) and predicate (*P*-term) classes are assumed to have at least one member, which is known as *the existential presupposition*. On the existential presupposition, for example, (I) sentences follow from (A) sentences, but not when that presupposition is not made. Hence, even with respect to immediate inference, there are two sets of logical relations, known as the *strong* and *weak* squares of opposition, whose respective differences depend upon whether the existential presupposition is adopted. The differences at stake here are commonly diagrammed in logic texts.

Logic, deductive. See also **arguments, deductive.**

Logic, extensional. Any system of logic that restricts its attention to truth-functional operators and truth-functional properties of and relations between sentences. Operators, properties, and relations of this kind are those for which semantically relevant features of language and logic are exclusively limited to functions of truth values (true/false) exclusively. Thus, when molecular sentences (of the form "It is not the case that . . . ," " ". . . or ____," ". . . and ____," and such) are interpreted truth-functionally, the only properties of their atomic components that make a difference to their own truth values are the truth values of those components and not whether they are related by meaning, causation, or whatever. Thus, when the conditional (or "if . . . then ____") connective is understood as a truth-functional connective, the only property of the ". . ." and of the "____" sentences that makes a difference to the truth or falsity of "if . . . then ____" sentences composed of them is their truth values, where such sentences are said to be true when either their "..." sentence is false or their "____" sentence is true. This interpretation is known as *the material conditional.* "If Babe Ruth is president, then two plus two equals four" and "If Babe Ruth is president, then two plus two does not equal four," for example, are both true under this interpretation, simply because Babe Ruth is not president. As truth-functions, universal generalizations are logically equivalent to a conjunction of n-members, whereas existential generalizations are logically equivalent to a disjunction of n-members, for any (finite) n-membered universe of discourse. While the rules of inference of extensional logics can establish the validity of a large class of arguments, arguments that appeal to non-truth-functional operators, properties of and relations between sentences (by taking into account possible definitional, causal, or other relations between them) lie beyond its scope and require consideration within other frameworks. See also **conditionals; logic, intensional.**

Logic, inductive. See also **inductive logic.**

Logic, intensional. Any system of logic that goes beyond merely truth-functional operators and truth-functional properties of and relations between sentences. Among the kinds of sentences that are studied within intensional logics are subjunctive conditionals, counterfactual conditionals, nomological conditionals, deontological conditionals, and others unnamed.

Logic, predicate. Any system of logic that analyzes the validity of arguments on the basis of the internal structure of sentences rather than treating them as basic units of analysis. Even the traditional argument, "All men are mortal; Socrates is a man; therefore, Socrates is mortal," cannot be successfully analysed within sentential logic, since it has the form, "p; q; therefore, r," where "p," "*q*," and "*r*" are variables standing for unspecified sentences, which is not a valid form. Within predicate logic, however, it can be analysed as having the form "$(x)(Hx \rightarrow Mx)$; Hs; therefore, Ms," where "Hx" means "*x* is a man (human)," "Mx" means "*x* is mortal," and "*s*" stands for "Socrates." When predicate logic is restricted to properties of and relations between individuals with no quantification over properties, it is known as "first order"; when quantification over properties is allowed, it is "second order" instead. Almost all investigations within contemporary logic go beyond predicate logic.

Logic, sentential. Any system of logic that restricts its attention to entire sentences, while ignoring the internal structure of the sentences themselves. See also **logic; logic, extensional; logic, predicate.**

Logical atomism. Advocated by **Bertrand Russell** and by Ludwig Wittgenstein, especially in his *Tractatus Logico-Philosophicus*, early in the twentieth century. According to this view, the external world and (first-order) predicate logic have the same structure, where the world is supposed to be composed of facts (arrangments of things or states of affairs), not of things (apart from their relations to other things). There are atomic facts corresponding to atomic propositions and molecular facts corresponding to molecular propositions. In Russell's version, atomic facts might be the objects of knowledge by acquaintance, thereby connecting ontology and epistemology. Both abandoned their positions, Wittgenstein introducing a new version of linguistic philosophy in his *Philosophical Investigations*, which emphasized the idea of asking not for the meaning of words but considering their use. In an introduction to the *Tractatus*, Russell observed that many of Wittgenstein's views could be explained by a failure to appreciate the **metalanguage/object-language**

distinction, according to which it is permissible to use one language (the metalanguage) to talk about another language (the object-language), which may have motivated, at least in part, his later views.

Logical consistency. A set of sentences is logically consistent provided it is logically possible for them to all be true together. This condition is often adopted as necessary for rationality of belief. Thus, whenever z believes that p and z believes whatever else must be true if p is true, then it is not the case that z believes any q, where not-p follows from q. This appears to be appropriate, since it should be logically possible that z's beliefs are all true together, but it has been criticized as too strong to be justifiable, especially by proponents of **naturalized epistemology.**

Logical positivism/logical empiricism. Closely related, influential philosophical movements that emerged between World Wars I and II. Logical positivism accepted the **analytic/synthetic distinction,** the **observational/ theoretical distinction,** and a methodological commitment to the use of extensional logic for philosophical explications. Sometimes it embraced the thesis that every meaningful non-analytic sentence is either an observation sentence or a deductive consequence of observation sentences, as in A. J. Ayer's *Language, Truth and Logic.* **Logical empiricism** succeeded **logical positivism** by abandoning this overly stringent conception of cognitive significance and, in some cases, by abandoning the **analytic/ synthetic distinction** or, in other cases, by abandoning the **observational/theoretical distinction.** Rudolf Carnap, one of the most important members of these movements, later abandoned even the methodological commitment to extensional languages as indispensable for philosophical explications. See also **analytic/synthetic**

distinction; explications; logic, extensional; observable/theoretical distinction; paradox of analysis.

Logical possibility/necessity/impossibility. A sentence S in a language L describes a logically possible (necessary, impossible) state of affairs or "world" in relation to L if and only if it is not the case that not-S follows from L (it is the case that S follows from L, it is the case that not-S follows from L) as a deductive consequence of logical truths or definitions that are true in L. In relation to ordinary English, for example, it is a logical possibility that a bachelor is a millionaire (it is a logical necessity that, if he is a bachelor, then he is unmarried; and it is a logical impossibility that, if he is a bachelor, then he is not unmarried), assuming satisfaction of the requirement of a uniform interpretation, where the same words have the same meaning throughout. See also **uniform interpretation, requirement of.**

Logical truth. Any instance of a logical form which has only true uniform interpretations is known as a logical truth. Often sentences that are true simply on the basis of their meaning or by virtue of definitions are also qualified as logical truths, because they are reducible to logical truths by substitution of definiens for definiendum. See also **analytic/synthetic distinction; a priori/a posteriori distinction; Quine, W. V. O.**

Lottery paradox. A set of inconsistent beliefs that arises—seemingly inescapably—if beliefs about outcomes with low probabilities are combined with a high-probability acceptance condition. When a lottery with ten tickets is fair, for example, then each ticket has only a probability of $1/10$ of winning. If acceptance requires a value of 0.5 or greater, then, for each of the ten tickets, it must be inferred that it will not win; yet, by hypothesis, the lottery is fair, which implies that one ticket will win.

A modest version of the lottery paradox obtains for two outcomes, such as heads or tails on the toss of a fair coin, when both outcomes have a probability of 0.5. If 0.5 is sufficient for acceptance, then both heads and tails should be accepted; if 0.5 is not sufficient for acceptance, then neither should be accepted. For any version with three or more outcomes with probabilities less than 0.5, the paradox will arise. In the theory of knowledge, the lottery paradox is often taken to establish that rational justification cannot be construed in terms of a high probability requirement for rational belief, since otherwise persons might be rationally justified in accepting inconsistent beliefs. This difficulty was first noted by Henry Kyburg, Jr. See also **acceptance and rejection rules; conjunctivitis.**

Luck, epistemic. A state of belief distinct from knowledge, which occurs when a person z claims to know that p, believes or accepts that p, and that p is the case, yet it would be wrong to say that z knows that p because z is not justified in that belief (or z does not have the right to believe that p). Alternatively, epistemic luck occurs when a person's beliefs, based upon superstition or hunch, turn out to be true, even though they are not—perhaps not even remotely—rationally justified (or justifiable).

M

Material conditionals. See **conditionals.**
Mathematical induction. Its name notwithstanding, mathematical induction is a special case of deductive reasoning. When something is true of a base case and is also true of any other member that belongs to the set of

things to which the base case belongs as a random or arbitrary member of that specific set, then it is true of everything that satisfies the condition of either being the base case or of belonging to the set to which it belongs.

Mathematics, pure vs. applied. Mathematics may be pursued as the study of formal systems, where applications of those formal systems are restricted to abstract domains. This is the area of *pure* mathematics. Mathematics may also be pursued as the study of formal systems where those systems are subject to empirical interpretations. This is the area of *applied* mathematics, which also qualifies as a branch of empirical science. Alternatively, the domain of mathematics can be restricted to comparative (or topological) relations and to quantitative (or metrical) relations exclusively. See also **formal systems; theories, standard conception of.**

Meaning analysis. A meaning analysis provides a report upon the established usage of a word, phrase, or expression within a language-using community. Since linguistic practices may differ from one community to another and from time to time, they are relative to those communities and times. The word "fuzz," for example, was slang for policemen or officers of the law to street gangs in New York during the 1960s. A sentence that formulates a meaning analysis will either be true or be false insofar as it provides an accurate or inaccurate report of the linguistic practices of the community and time. Alternatively, it is a dictionary definition.

Meaningfulness, problem of (also known as the problem of cognitive significance). The conundrum of establishing criteria for distinguishing between meaningful and meaningless assertions. The principle of **verifiability** was advanced as a solution to this problem by **logical positivism,** but it was too stringent and excluded many kinds of sentences the meaningfulness of which was not in doubt. That principle was abandoned by **logical empiricism** in favor of decidedly more liberal standards, especially that of empirical testability, in the case of synthetic sentences. This problem must be distinguished from the **problem of demarcation.**

Memory. Mental faculty for the retention of beliefs. Sometimes a distinction is drawn between short-term and long-term memory. Since what different persons seem to remember very often conflicts, memory turns out to be a disputed potential source of knowledge or justification. See also **introspection.**

Metalanguage/object-language. A relative distinction between any language and the language used to talk about that language. When the meaning of a sentence in French is discussed in English, then French is the **object-language** and English is the **metalanguage.** See also **truth, semantic conception of.**

Metaphysics. Traditionally understood to be the study of the most general properties of the physical world, but including human minds and every other kind of being. It is sometimes referred to as "ontology." Alternatively, the term has been used to contrast meaningless or "metaphysical" theories with meaningful or "scientific" hypotheses. Metaphysics, epistemology, and axiology (also known as value theory) are perhaps the three most basic divisions of philosophy, as it is traditionally understood.

Mill's methods. A set of principles of inductive inference advanced by John Stuart Mill. These include (1) the *method of agreement*, whereby a property that has been observed to be present whenever a certain effect is present, while other observed properties have sometimes been present and sometimes absent, is tentatively supposed to be causally connected to that effect, perhaps as a sufficient condition; (2) the *method of difference,* whereby a property that has been observed to be absent when the effect is absent and present when the effect is present, whereas other observed properties have sometimes been present and sometimes been absent when that effect has been present and absent, is tentatively supposed to be causally connected to that effect, perhaps as a necessary condition; and (3) the *method of concomitant variation,* whereby a property that has been observed to be systematically related to the occurrence of an event, such that the presence of that event varies with the presence of that property, is tentatively supposed to be causally connected to that effect, perhaps as a necessary and sufficient condition. When they are utilized together with systematic controlled experiments across suitably varied conditions, these principles may support highly sophisticated inferences about **causation.**

Models/theories. Models are usually simplifications or abstractions of the phenomena within some domain. Models of the world that are constructed by science are commonly referred to as **theories** without implying that they must be incomplete or untrue. Philosophers engage in the construction of models as **explications.** The **philosophy of science** can be viewed as devoted to constructing models of science.

Model theory/proof theory. Model theory studies possible interpretations of formal systems, especially with respect to relations of **semantic entailment. Proof theory** studies their syntax and corresponding relations of **syntactic derivability.** See also **formal systems; theories.**

Modus ponens. A deductive principle of inference that permits the derivation of a conclusion of the form "*q*" from premises of the form, "If p then q" and "p." Given "if p then q" and "p," infer "q."

Modus tollens. A deductive principle of inference that permits the derivation of a conclusion of the form "not-p" from premises of the form, "If p then q" and "not-q." Given "if p then q" and "not-q," infer "not-p."

Motivating reasons. Those factors that cause a person to believe or to accept a proposition independently of whether those factors properly qualify as grounds, reasons, or evidence in accordance with appropriate standards of reasoning. Alternatively, any faculty or capacity that causes a person to accept a belief without concern for its normative rationality.

N

Naturalism. Characterizes any version of naturalized epistemology. Alternatively, any attempt to prove the existence of God on the basis of observations about the world or concerning the course of natural events.

Naturalized epistemology. Any of the positions defined by one or another of the following views: (1) *the replacement thesis* that the only meaningful questions are those that can be answered on the basis of the methods of inquiry employed by science (Quine); (2) *the transformational thesis* that, although some questions not answerable by scientific methods are still meaningful, whether anyone ever knows anything is properly determined by scientific inquiries into the causal and neurobiological mechanisms that bring about our beliefs (Goldman); and (3) *the traditional thesis* that the most privileged and reliable methods for acquiring an understanding of the world are the methods that are used by science (Rescher).

Nomic/nomological. Ordinarily used as a synonym for lawful. Any non-logical necessary connection or causal relation involving **laws of nature** is a nomic or nomological connection or relation. Most importantly, what is described by a sentence is *nomically possible* if its occurrence would not violate the laws of nature, *nomically necessary* if its non-occurrence would violate the laws of nature, and *nomically impossible* if its occurrence would violate the laws of nature. See also **physical possibility/ necessity/impossibility.**

Nomic expectability. The degree to which an explanandum could have been expected to occur, in relation to the antecedent conditions and the general laws that brought it about. In Hempel's **covering-law model of explanation,** for example, explanations are understood as arguments that display the nomic expectability of the occurrence of their explanandum events, outcomes, or phenomena, given those general laws and other conditions.

Nomic relevance. A predicate is nomically relevant to the truth of a lawlike sentence when it designates a property whose presence or absence makes a difference to the occurrence of the outcome attribute. All causally relevant properties are nomically relevant, but all nomically relevant properties are causally relevant only if there are no non-causal laws.

Nomic responsibility. The conditions that were responsible for bringing an event, outcome, or phenomenon about in accordance with **laws of nature.** In the **causal-relevance model of explanation,** explanations are understood to be arguments that display the covering laws and other conditions that were nomically responsible for the occurrence of the explanandum-phenomenon.

Nominal definition. A nominal definition occurs when some new word, phrase, or expression is introduced as having the same meaning as some old word, phrase, or expression. Thus, the word "tiglon" could be introduced into English to have the same meaning as the phrase, "offspring of a male tiger and a female lion," as Hempel observes, where the acceptability of this definition is only a matter of agreement between the members of the relevant language-using community. The definiendum and the definiens have the same meaning simply as a matter of stipulation. Alternatively, defining the meaning of a word as a matter of convention.

Nominalism vs. realism. These are positions on the existence of what are known as universals, which now tend to be viewed as properties that can be instantiated by more than one thing. In the Middle Ages, nominalism was the view that everything is particular, the only universals being words. Nominalism and realism were both opposed to conceptualism, and there were two importantly different versions of realism (Aristotelian and Platonic). According to contemporary versions of nominalism, there is no more to any universal than its class of instances. Thus, every property that has the same class of instances is the same property, and every property that has no instances is identical. The classes of unicorns and of werewolves are therefore one and the same. According to contemporary realism, there is more to a universal than its class of instances, and it is not the case that universals that have the same class of instances are the same property. But it should be observed that the term **realism** occurs in various senses.

Non-defeasibility condition. Any requirement added to the definition of knowledge as justified true belief that is intended to block the admissibility of

Gettier-style counterexamples. A condition of this kind might maintain, for example, that any acceptable justification for a belief must itself be non-defeasible, which would mean that there must be no true proposition such that, were it added to any such justification, then that person would no longer be justified in accepting such a belief.

Normal science. See also **Kuhn, Thomas S.**

O

Objectivity/subjectivity distinction. Properties whose presence or absence depends upon and varies with different observers or thinkers are said to be *subjective*, while those that do not vary in this way or remain the same in relation to a framework or a fixed point of view are said to be *objective*. Alternatively, properties of the external world that exist apart from any human minds are said to be objective, while those whose presence depends on the existence of human minds are said to be subjective.

Observable/theoretical distinction. Traditional distinction between properties (or predicates that refer to properties) that are directly accessible to sense experience and those that are not. It can be drawn in several different ways. One is to define *observable properties* as properties whose presence or absence can be directly ascertained, under suitable conditions, by means of direct observation; *theoretical properties* are then defined as non-observational. Alternatively, a distinction is drawn between *observable, dispositional,* and *theoretical* predicates, where observable predicates describe observable properties of observable entities; dispositional predicates describe unobservable properties of observable entities; and theoretical predicates describe unobservable properties of unobservable entities. As Rudolf Carnap has observed, scientists tend to use the notion of observation somewhat more broadly than do philosophers, characterizing as "observable" any properties whose presence or absence can be ascertained, under suitable conditions, by direct observation or by relatively simple measurement. There are no decisive reasons for preferring one of these definitions to the others, as long as any ambiguities are resolved as they arise. See also **basic statements; direct perception; dispositions; fallibilism.**

Observation. See also **observable/theoretical distinction; perception.**

Occam's Razor. A methodological maxim that is attributed to William of Occam, which asserts that entities should not be multiplied beyond necessity: "It is in vain to do by many what could be done by fewer!" Occam's Razor suggests that simpler theories should be preferred to more complex theories. Simpler theories are generally preferable, however, only when other things (such as their respective clarity, scope, and power) are equal.

Omniscience. The property of knowing everything that can be known. Alternatively, a person z would be omniscient if and only if, for every proposition p that is true in any universe of discourse, z knows that p. Omniscience, omnipotence, and benevolence are often viewed as attributes of God.

Ontic/epistemic. Indicates a difference between kinds of questions that arise in philosophical contexts. Ontic questions concern what is the case (truth) and merely epistemic what we take to be the case (beliefs).

Although the nature of truth is an ontic question on correspondence theories, it becomes an epistemic question on pragmatic accounts. Some positions are defined by combinations of ontic and epistemic theses. An ontic answer to an epistemic question (or vice versa) normally commits a **category mistake**. See also **realism, classic; realism, scientific.**

Ontological argument. See also **Anslem, Saint.**

Ontology/epistemology. Among the most central domains of philosophical inquiry. Ontology (sometimes called **metaphysics**) aims at discovering a framework for understanding the kinds of things that constitute the world's structure, and **epistemology** aims at discovering the principles by means of which the world's properties might be known.

Operational definitions. Attempts to reduce the meaning of words to their criteria of application. See also **meaningfulness, problem of; ontic/epistemic reduction sentences.**

Ordinary language, appeal to. Any attempt to establish grounds, reasons, or evidence in support of a position by citing the ordinary use of ordinary language. A presumption embedded in this approach is that ordinary language manifests all the distinctions that are relevant to (or that make a difference to) philosophical arguments. The more technical the subject, therefore, the less plausible the appeal. Some philosophers maintain that departures from ordinary language are the source of philosophical confusion and that philosophical problems ought to disappear once we properly understand ordinary language. Ordinary philosophers in this sense include Gilbert Ryle, J. L. Austin, and the later Wittgenstein.

Orthodox statistical hypothesis testing. The theory of statistical hypothesis testing developed by R. A.

Fisher, Jerzy Neyman, and Egon Pearson, which is widely utilized, especially in the behavioral sciences. Among philosophers, this theory is defended by Ronald Giere and Deborah Mayo.

Ostensive definition. Words are "defined" ostensively by displaying samples or examples of things of the kind that is thereby defined. The meaning of the word "chair," for example, could be explained by showing some chairs to somebody. Ostensive definition provides a means for relating words to things without reliance upon other words, which means that, strictly speaking, ostensive definitions are only "definitions" in an extended sense. One risk involved in their use is that properties of the examples (such as the color, size, and shape of an overstuffed chair) might be taken to be properties of every thing of the kind defined (such as being a chair).

P

Paradigm. See also **Kuhn, Thomas S.**

Paradox of analysis. The apparently contradictory requirements necessary for an adequate conceptual analysis, namely: that the concept to be defined must be identical with the defining concept (and therefore be interchangeable while preserving truth values) and that the defining concept must add something that goes beyond the original (since otherwise analysis would be pointless). Alternatively, a conundrum alleged to confront the conception of analytic philosophy as an attempt to match definiens to definienda in arriving at suitable definitions, namely: either we know what we are talking about, in which case analytic philosophy is unnecessary; or we do not know what we are talking about, in which case it is impossible. But either we know what we are talking about or we do not. Thus, either analytic philosophy is unnecessary or it is impossible. It appears to be resolvable when philosophical analyses are understood as **explications,** where we begin with partial or incomplete understanding.

Peirce, Charles S. (1839–1914). A very important American philosopher, was a student of metaphysics and epistemology. The originator of the theory of signs (or "semiotic"), Peirce was the first and greatest of the classic pragmatists (the others being **William James** and **John Dewey**) and elaborated a model of science as a process of **abduction** built on the principle of **inference to the best explanation.** He is also known for defining "truth" as the opinion that the community of scientific inquirers would converge upon if inquiry were conducted indefinitely. Apparently Peirce thought that inquiry would continue indefinitely and that every question about the world accessible to science would be settled, but not with certainty. Thus, he also advocated **fallibilism** by maintaining that any belief, no matter how strongly confirmed, ought to be viewed as subject to revision and to possible rejection on the basis of future experience.

Percept. Any complex of sensations in virtue of which a physical object is perceived. A constellation of sensations of colors, shapes, and sizes might be perceived as a chessboard with its pieces in the opening position.

Perception (or observation). The act of perceiving (or observing) or the act of acquiring percepts as the appearances of things that might or might not exist independently of the subject having that perceptual experience. Alternatively, the interpretation of experience by the use of language to describe the contents of experience. The incorrigibility (or fallibility) of perception (observation) is a critical issue in epistemology.

Perception, causal theory of. Any theory, based in part on the argument from illusion, that asserts that what we directly perceive in acts of perception are the appearances of things and that the properties of objects must be indirectly inferred or logically constructed as either the causes of appearances or as constructs out of sense data. Alternatively, the view that perception arises as a result of causal interactions between perceivers and things perceived, about which our knowledge may only be indirect. See also **illusion, argument from.**

Perception, direct realist theory of. The view that we have direct access to how things are in the external world though perception. The direct realist theory of perception is commonly described as "naive."

Perception, phenomenalist theory of. The view that we only perceive the appearances of things as they arise in experience, given we have no reason to believe that there exists an external world beyond experience to which we can appeal to explain it. Alternatively, the external world is simply a cognitive construct from the appearances available to us through experience, where its independent existence can never be known. See also **idealism, Kantian.**

Phenomenalism. See also **Perception, phenomenalist theory of.**

Philosophy of science. Attempt to reconstruct the principles by means of which the pursuit of **science** might be possible as an activity whose methods are suitable to attain its goals, since otherwise the pursuit of science cannot properly be regarded as a rational activity. Alternatively, the goal of the philosophy of science is to build a model of science, employing especially the method of explication to such concepts as law, theory, and explanation. Among the most important models of science are **inductivism, deductivism, abductivism,** and **Bayesianism.** Some philosophers, including **Kuhn, Lakatos,** and Laudan, study science as a process and emphasize historical case studies, while others, such as Carnap, **Hempel,** and **Salmon,** tend to study science as a product, emphasizing logical analysis. On naturalistic approaches, philosophy of science may be viewed as an attempt to describe the practices of the members of the scientific community. See also **history of science; naturalized epistemology.**

Philosophy of science, feminist. Any study of science as a process or as a product that emphasizes the importance of considerations of gender to a proper understanding. Various feminist positions can be distinguished, ranging from the view that traditional conceptions of scientific method are inherently defective because they have been developed by men (as in the work of Evelyn Fox Keller and Ruth Hubbard) to the view that sometimes the results of the application of scientific methods have yielded theories about women that are inaccurate and misleading, which most theoreticians of science would not dispute. Others fall in between, advancing such ideas as that good empiricists should be good feminists (Lynn Nelson) or that, as Paul Feyerabend has proposed, in science anything goes (Sandra Harding).

Physical possibility/necessity/impossibility. A sentence S in a language L describes a physically possible (necessary, impossible) state of affairs or "world" in relation to L and the set of lawlike sentences N that is true of the world if and only if it is not the case that not-S follows from L-and-N (it is the case that S follows from L-and-N, but not from L alone, it is the case that not-S follows from

L-and-*N*, but not from *L* alone). In relation to technical English and Newton's laws, for example, it is a physical possibility for an object to continue its motion in a straight line or remain at rest (it is a physical necessity that, if an object is not affected by an external force, then it will continue its motion in a straight line or remain at rest; it is a physical impossibility that, if an object is not affected by an external force, it will not continue its motion in a straight line or remain at rest). See also **nomic/nomological.**

Plato (427–347 B.C.). Greek philosopher who was a student of Socrates and teacher of Aristotle. Among the most important thinkers in the history of philosophy, Plato introduced a *Theory of Forms,* according to which every thing in the world is a (possibly imperfect) instance of corresponding eternal and unchanging Forms. By distinguishing between the *World of Being,* which includes the Forms and truths of mathematics, and the *World of Becoming,* which includes the ordinary things of daily experience (such as animals and plants) as well as their transitory effects (including shadows and reflections), he maintained that objects in the World of Being could be known, while objects in the World of Becoming could (at best) be subjects of opinion. Plato also suggested that there were grades or degrees of reality, where shadows and reflections were among the lowest grade, animals and plants the next lowest, truths of mathematics the next highest, and Forms the highest. He held that human beings had distinct faculties that afford access to these distinct kinds of things, thereby integrating psychology, epistemology, and ontology. Plato thus embaces a conception of certainty as a necessary condition of knowledge, but it is an ontological property rooted in the nature of the things known rather than a psychological property rooted in the nature of the knowing thing, as in the case of Descartes. He also advanced the theory of *knowledge as recollection,* according to which every human mind participates in the Eternal Mind before birth. Although as a consequence every human mind knows everything there is to know before birth, the trauma of birth induces forgetfulness, which can be overcome by experiences that bring specific items of knowledge back to mind. Plato thereby endorsed innate or inborn knowledge.

Popper, Karl R. (1902–   ). British philosopher of science, best known for his conception of science as a process of conjectures and (attempted) refutations and for his discussions of the growth of scientific knowledge. Also contributed to the propensity interpretation of probability and to the study of laws of nature, of dispositions and of scientific theories. See also **conjectures and refutations; demarcation, problem of; falsifiability.**

Possibility/necessity/impossibility, historical. See **historical possibility/necessity/impossibility.**

Possibility/necessity/impossibility, logical. See **logical possibility/necessity/impossibility.**

Possibility/necessity/impossibility, physical. See **physical possibility/necessity/impossibility.**

Pragmatics. The study of the relations between signs, what they stand for, and sign users. Alternatively, the study of the relations between words, what they stand for, and word users. Alternatively, any study that involves essential reference to the purpose (or motive) that causes us to act as we do.

Pragmatism. Theory of knowledge adopted by a number of American philosophers (especially **Charles Peirce, William James, John Dewey,** and C. I. Lewis) and later refined by various contemporary philosophers as neopragmatists (**W. V. O. Quine,** Nicholas Rescher, and Richard Rorty). Classic pragmatists tend to maintain the following eight theses: (1) beliefs and systems of beliefs are instruments; (2) the acceptability of a belief or a system of beliefs is ultimately a function of the extent to which those beliefs allow for successful adaptation; (3) all beliefs or systems of beliefs, including mathematical beliefs, are fallible; (4) some of our knowledge concerns an external world which exists apart from any human minds; (5) the only process for evaluating beliefs about the external world is the method or methods of the natural sciences; (6) the truth or rationality of a belief depends on its predictive utility in coping with future experience; (7) the most successful predictive beliefs or systems of belief yield epistemically privileged descriptions of the world; and (8) hypotheses about the world are to be regarded as true if they are warrantedly assertible (or "authorizable") under the rules of acceptance embedded in the methods of science. Pragmatists, however, may disagree over the justifiability of belief in the existence of abstract, unobservable, or theoretical entities. Peirce and James, for example, allowed for such beliefs, while Dewey thought the methods of science precluded belief in objects with causal powers that were not observable.

Predicate logic. See logic, predicate.

Prediction. Anticipating the course of future experience. When a prediction is supported by evidence, it may qualify as rational. When it is not supported by evidence, it may be referred to as a prophecy. Also, predictions in science are characteristically conditional, while prophecies are characteristically unconditional. An important problem in the philosophy of science is the relationship between predictions and explanations.

Presuppositions. Propositions that must be true for some other proposition to be either true or false. For example, what are known as leading (or as "complex") questions have presuppositions that may beg the question at issue. If there were no external world, for example, the question, "Is the external world entirely composed of physical things?", would have no answer (neither the proposition that it is nor the proposition that it is not would be true), because it has a false presupposition.

Primary vs. secondary qualities. A distinction between properties whose existence does not depend upon the existence of any minds (the primary qualities) and those whose existence does depend upon the existence of some mind (the secondary qualities). The empiricists, especially Locke, **Berkeley,** and **Hume,** debated over the nature of and the extent to which properties are primary or secondary. According to phenomenalistic conceptions such as Berkeley's, every property turns out to be secondary, because nothing is supposed to exist apart from its perception by some perceiving thing. Classic examples of primary properties are the sizes and shapes of things, while their colors and textures (or "feels") are secondary properties. Some theories about natural laws make them mind-dependent as well. See also **Berkeley, Bishop George.**

Principal Principle, Lewis's. A principle advanced by **David Lewis,** which asserts that a person's degree of belief (or subjective credibility) in the proposition that A must always equal the objective probability (or the "chance") of A when it is known. Even given this principle, Lewis suggests that only subjectivists can fully appreciate the nature of objective chance.

Private knowledge. See also **knowledge, private.**

Probability, classic interpretation of. The probability of an outcome B in relation to conditions of kind A equals the number of possible outcomes of that kind divided by the number of possible outcomes under those conditions. With an ordinary coin, for example, the classic probability for heads would equal the number of possible outcomes of heads divided by the number of possible outcomes or 1/2. With a two-headed coin, it would equal $2/2 = 1$. Inspired by games of chance where the conditions for its application are often satisfied, its appeal is limited by the realization that coins can be bent, dice can be loaded, decks of cards can be abnormal, and the like, which indicates that the mere number of possible outcomes of kind B divided by the number of possible outcomes is not a generally reliable measure of the probability for that outcome. A more adequate conception would appeal instead to relevance relations.

Probability, frequency interpretation of. The probability of an outcome B in relation to conditions A equals the limiting frequency for outcomes of kind B within an infinite sequence of kind A. There are two principal varieties of frequency interpretations. (1) According to the *actual* frequency interpretation, an infinite sequence of kind A must exist for the corresponding probabilities to exist. Thus, if the world's history is merely finite, then no probabilities can exist as features of the world. (2) According to the *hypothetical* frequency interpretation, these probabilities are what the limiting frequencies would be or would have been if such a sequence were to occur or were to have occurred. The residual problem thus becomes one of justifying the values of these probabilities.

Probability, interpretations of. Any interpretation of the principles of probability. In view of the variety of different axiomatizations of mathematical probabilities, however, this should be broadly construed to encompass measures that satisfy principles of summation, of addition and of multiplication, whether or not they qualify as conditional probabilities in the technical sense. As Paul Humphreys has observed, interpretations of probabilities such as propensity conceptions that incorporate causal directedness (from causes to effects) cannot satisfy symmetrical requirements, such as definitions of conditional probabilities for which $P(B/A) = P(A\&B)/P(A) = P(A/B) \cdot P(B)/P(A) = P(B/A) \cdot P(A)/P(A)$. For if A is a cause and B is its effect, then even when there is a probability from A to B, there will generally not exist a corresponding probability from B to A. Alternatively, the phrase, "interpretation of probability," may be restricted to only those interpretations that satisfy classic theorems, such as Bayes's theorem, which require symmetry, in addition to principles such as those mentioned already, in which case the phrase, "conception of probability," may be used to refer to interpretations that are not symmetrical notions. The most important conceptions of probability are the **classic, frequency, logical, personal, propensity,** and **subjective interpretations.**

Probability, logical interpretation of. Any interpretation according to which probability is a relation between sentences that measure degrees of evidential support. John Maynard Keynes was an early advocate of such an approach. In later developments elaborated by Rudolf Carnap, logical probabilities represent relations of partial support that are characterized as degrees of entailment. Alternative theories of logical probability include those that identify them with degrees of nomic expectability, which can be found in both covering-law and causal-relevance models of explanation. Although Hempel originally envisioned the logical probability that relates an explanans to its explanandum in an I-S explanation as a degree of support in Carnap's sense, he subsequently abandoned that conception in favor of their identification with degrees of nomic expectability. Thus, statistical explanations no longer satisfy a requirement of total evidence but an alternative requirement of maximal specificity. A similar difference endures with the causal-relevance conception. See also **explanation.**

Probability, personal interpretation of. Any interpretation of the principles of probability according to which degrees of belief qualify as probabilities. This is a Bayesian conception for which the conditions that must be satisfied for some agent to possess rationality of belief are those of coherence, (sometimes) strict coherence, and conditionalization. There is widespread disagreement between Bayesians of different persuasions as to the relations that need to obtain between personal probabilities as subjective degrees of belief and physical probabilities as objective properties of the world. According to the Principal Principle advanced by David Lewis, for example, one's personal degree of belief in the proposition that p should equal the objective chance that p, whenever that chance happens to be known. While this suggests that personal probabilities and objective chances are closely related, some of those who favor personal probabilities dispense with objective chances altogether, and those who believe in objective chances are not thereby committed to personal probabilities. In particular, there is an important difference between degrees of belief and probabilistic beliefs, where probabilistic beliefs (about objective chances) require acceptance and rejection rules, while degrees of belief (on the personalist interpretation) do not.

Probability, propensity interpretation of. Any interpretation according to which probabilities are regarded as dispositions that are amenable to varying degrees of strength. There are two principal versions of the propensity interpretation, both of which depend upon the notion of an experimental arrangement (or of a "chance set-up"). According to the *long-run* version, which is developed in the work of **Peirce, Popper,** and Hacking, among others, propensities are dispositions to produce particular outcomes with characteristic limiting frequencies over infinite sequences of trials with appropriate chance set-ups. According to the *single-case* version, propensities are instead strengths of dispositions to produce one or another outcome on each single trial with those set-ups. Different versions of the single-case interpretation are found in the work of Mellor, Fetzer, and Railton. Most of their disagreements hinge upon important questions of semantics. On the long-run or the single-case approach, propensities are causes that produce frequencies as their effects and are not those frequencies themselves. The causal-relevance theory of explanation is based upon the single-case view.

Probability, subjective interpretation of. Any interpretation of probability as a degree of belief, whether or not it satisfies the mathematical relations of the calculus of probability. This approach is ordinarily introduced only to differentiate the normative constraints of the personalist interpretation from the descriptive character of the subjective interpretation. Although coherence and (sometimes) strict coherence, for example, are conditions that must be satisfied on their personal interpretation, neither is a necessary condition on a subjective interpretation, which permits incoherent degrees of belief. Alternatively, "subjective" and "personal" can be used as synonyms for the personal interpretation of probability.

Problem of Criteria. See also **criteria, the power of.**

Problem of demarcation. See also **demarcation, the power of.**

Problem of induction. See also **induction, the problem of.**

Problem of induction, new. See also **induction, the new problem of**.

Projectible predicates. The new problem of induction arises from the notion that some predicates are suitable for making predictions about future cases, while others are not. "Blue" and "green" appear to be projectible, for example, but **Goodman** introduced a new family of predicates, such as "grue" and "bleen," that are definable by means of projectible predicates but do not appear to be projectible. The new problem thus seems to be the old problem defined by **Hume** but appearing now in a new (linguistic) guise. A simple example of the problem might consist in reports about the color of emeralds, which have all been made prior to some time *t*, which, let us assume, might be midnight tonight. Even if all of the emeralds we have observed have been *green*, **Goodman** suggests, that affords no guarantee that they must remain that color in the future. Our evidence, for example, is consistent with the hypothesis that they might turn blue (or yellow, . . .) at midnight. What he has discovered is that we have been ignoring whole families of alternative hypotheses, such as that all emeralds are *grue*, where a thing is grue just in case it is observed before *t* and green or not observed before *t* and blue. Notice that, in terms of the language of grue, things that change from green to blue at midnight tonight actually remain the same color. So the new problem of induction is that of justifying our choice of one language framework rather than another. Why assume that any emeralds that were not observed before *t* are green rather than grue?

Proof theory/model theory. See also **model theory/ proof theory.**

Propositions. That which declarative sentences assert to be the case. (On the Fregean definition, a proposition is the thought expressed by a declarative sentence.) Also said to be the meaning of a sentence or the state of affairs it describes. Alternatively, an equivalence class of sentences where every sentence says the same thing (or has the same meaning).

Propositional knowledge. See also **knowledge, propositional.**

Provisoes. Clauses or articles that introduce conditions. On views such as the semantic conception of theories, theories are counterfactual idealizations that describe behavior under atypical conditions, such as the attraction between bodies when acted upon by gravitational forces exclusively. As Hempel has observed, this means that predictive and explanatory inferences based upon that theory must be accompanied by special clauses (or "provisoes") asserting that no other conditions are present in any specific instance of its application or for that theory to be subjected to empirical tests that might confirm or disconfirm it. Establishing that these conditions—which may involve observable or nonobservable properties—are satisfied is the "problem of provisoes".

Q

Quine, W. V. O. (1908–   ). An American philosopher and logician, perhaps best known for his critique of the **analytic/synthetic distinction,** for defending a sophisticated version of nominalism, for emphasizing the underdetermination of theories by evidence, and for the thesis of the indeterminacy of translation. See also **analytic/synthetic distinction; Duhem thesis; theories, underdetermination of; translation, indeterminacy of.**

R

Rationalism. Generally, this position maintains that there exists some knowledge (or rational beliefs) that we have not learned or otherwise acquired by sense experience or by direct or indirect inferences from what we have learned or acquired by sense experience. Some rationalists, such as Plato and Descartes, assert the strong view that there is such a thing as knowledge, but that it cannot be based upon or otherwise derived from sense experience. Other rationalists, especially Kant, maintain that there are other sources of knowledge, such as knowledge that is **synthetic** and **a posteriori** or **analytic** and **a priori,** while asserting the existence of **synthetic a priori knowledge.** Alternatively, the thesis that some knowledge, possibly including knowledge of language or of the categories of thought, is either genetic, innate, or inborn, or else any position that asserts the existence of **synthetic a priori knowledge.**

Rationality, Bayesian conception of. See also **Bayesianism.**

Rationality of action. See also **action, rational.**

Rationality of belief. See also **belief, rational.**

Realism. Asserts that there is an external world and that some of our beliefs about such a world are true and that we can (sometimes) determine which of those beliefs are true. Realism in this sense is compatible with **instru-**

mentalism/neo-instrumentalism, when such views are interpreted as affirming the existence of an external world that is describable by observable predicates but not by theoretical ones. See also **observable/theoretical distinction.**

Realism, blind. A theory advanced by Robert Almeder that accepts the first and second tenets of **classic realism** and of **classic scientific realism** while denying the third. It therefore denies that we have any reliable decision procedure for selecting or determining which of our beliefs succeeds in some important measure in describing the external world. As such, it is properly understood as a form of **instrumentalism** asserting the first two conditions of classic realism and of classic scientific realism.

Realism, classic. Asserts (1) that we inhabit a world whose nature and existence is neither logically nor causally dependent upon any mind; (2) that some of our beliefs about this world are accurate, even if incomplete, descriptions, and thereby qualify as true; and (3) that our methods of inquiry enable us to discover that (at least) some of our beliefs about the world are true. Weaker versions deny that classic realism requires a commitment to any definition of truth, even though it does require some conception of accurate descriptions of an external world. By comparison, stronger versions would assert that our methods of inquiry are infallible, completely reliable, or effective decision procedures.

Realism, classic scientific. Maintains (1) that we inhabit a world whose nature and existence is neither logically nor causally dependent on any mind, (2) that some of our beliefs about this world—including theoretical beliefs concerning unobservable entities that we interpret to have causal effects of which we occasionally become aware through experience—are accurate, even if incomplete, descriptions, and thereby qualify as true, and

(3) that our methods of inquiry enable us to discover that (at least) some of our beliefs about the world—including some which are theoretical—are true. There are weaker and stronger versions, as in the case of **classic realism.**

Realism/nominalism. See also **nominalism vs. realism.**

Realism, Platonic. Maintains that there are transcendent, immaterial, unchanging, and eternal essences of which everything that exists within the world is a (possibly imperfect) instance. In Plato's *Theory of Forms,* these objects (known as "Forms") and mathematical theorems are the only proper objects of *knowledge,* where beliefs about the temporary and changing world accessible to sense experience can (at best) qualify as *opinions.*

Realism, scientific. The view that the theoretical (or "hypothetical") entities that are characterized by a true theory actually exist even though they cannot be directly observed. Alternatively, that the evidence that confirms a theory also serves to confirm the existence of any theoretical or "hypothetical" entities characterized by that theory. While realism has traditionally been couched in terms of the **observable/theoretical distinction,** its adequacy, unlike that of **instrumentalism/neo-instrumentalism,** does not depend upon the tenability of any such distinction.

Reality. Everything there is. Alternatively, what would be described by a complete set of true sentences (including every sentence that is true and no sentence that is false) in an ideal language, if such a thing were possible.

Reason. The faculty or capacity for the kind of thinking known as reasoning, often thought to be distinctive to humans. Reasoning, in turn, characterizes the ability to have or give reasons for accepting beliefs (as "theoretical" reasoning) or for making decisions (as "practical" reasoning). The study of theoretical reasoning is pursued in **epistemology, logic,** and **philosophy of science,** practical reasoning in **decision** theory.

Reasons. Anything that can serve as grounds or evidence for anything else, especially relative to the acceptance and rejection of beliefs or to the adoption of a decision or not. Some reasons can take the form of experiences, such as when your reason for thinking that someone was somewhere is because you saw him there. Other reasons take the form of descriptions, some of which may characterize experience, but some of which may have the standing of analytic rather than synthetic sentences or which may describe generalizations transcending immediate experience. Alternatively, that which causes a person to believe what they believe without thereby justifying that belief. Since brainwashing, for example, might qualify as a reason, it should be observed that having a reason differs from having a good reason. See also **criteria, the problem of.**

Reductionism. Any attempt to reduce, replace, or derive theories of one (higher) level to, by, or from those of another (lower) level qualifies as a form of reductionism. The most important instances include attempts to reduce the mind to the body, the intensional to the extensional, the theoretical to the observable, and the external world to sense data. Alternatively, any attempt to reduce what is complex to what is simple, largely driven by the spirit of Occam's Razor. Though enormously influential, no reduction of any of these kinds appears to have been successful, in spite of repeated efforts to work them out. See also **Occam's Razor.**

Reduction sentences. A device introduced by Carnap to deal with the problem of defining dispositional predicates. The term "hunger," for example, might appear to be definable by specifying an observable test condition (such as the presence of food) and an observable response (eating that food). On this approach, "x is hungry" means "if x is given food, then x eats that food." Interpreted as a material conditional, however, this definition of "x is hungry" becomes synonymous with "either x is not given food, or x eats that food," which turns out to be true of black chairs, stone walls, etc., whenever they are not given food. To avoid this problem, Carnap proposed making definitions "partial" and "relative to" those test conditions. Thus, a *unilateral* reduction sentence for "hunger" might state, "if x is given food, then if x eats that food, then x is hungry," and a *bilateral* reduction sentence for that same term might state, "if x is given food, then x is hungry if and only if x eats that food." These definitions are only partial since, in cases in which the test condition is not satisfied, the applicability or not of that term remains indeterminate, even though (presumably) the entity under consideration is hungry or is not. Moreover, as **Goodman** has observed, any term introduced by means of a reduction sentence, strictly speaking, is not eliminable in favor of some other word, phrase, or expression, and thus actually occurs as a primitive. Other approaches have gone beyond methodological commitments to extensional (or "truth-functional") logic by appealing to subjunctive and to causal conditionals, which seem to be required to find an adequate solution.

Reichenbach, Hans (1891–1953). German-American philosopher of science who taught at UCLA, best known for his work on space/time and probability and induction. See also **vindication, pragmatic.**

Reliabilism. The thesis that whether anyone knows anything at all depends upon whether their true beliefs have been brought about by a reliable belief-producing method, mechanism, or process (typically, one that is functioning normally under standard conditions). Philosophers who endorse this position, however, fall into two different groups. The first group adopts the reliability condition as a *condition of justification* (or as an addendum to a condition of justification) for knowledge. These philosophers insist that justification is necessary for knowledge but that justification depends upon the reliability of the belief-producing mechanism, method, or process that brings a belief about. They may or may not maintain that justification requires a knower to recognize that such a belief has been reliably produced or, under suitable conditions, to be able to specify what makes that method, mechanism, or process reliable. Those who insist that these conditions of recognition and specification be satisfied are advocates of **internalism,** while those who deny that such conditions are necessary are advocates of **externalism** instead. The second group maintains that the reliability condition is *not* a condition of justification and that, while knowledge does require true beliefs that are reliably produced (of which a person may or may not be aware), it does *not* require justification. The defense for this position is rooted in the view of justification as a reason-giving activity which is not necessary for beliefs to be reliably produced. These thinkers therefore accept a reliability theory of knowledge even though they reject a reliability theory of justification. Whether a philosopher belongs to the first or to the second of these groups, however, to determine whether someone knows something necessarily requires determining whether their beliefs were caused by or were brought about by reliable belief-producing methods, mechanisms, or processes. To the extent to which these methods, mechanisms, and processes are those of perception, memory, and other

121

human abilities and capacities, determinations of reliability tend to fall into the domain of psychologists, neurobiologists, and cognitive scientists, generally. But this implies that central questions in the theory of knowledge can only be answered by or on the basis of research conducted by inquiries that fall within the scope of natural science. Reliabilism thus appears to be highly compatible with or even a species of at least one variety of **naturalized epistemology.**

Reliability. The property of a method, mechanism, or process by virtue of which it tends to produce true beliefs rather than false beliefs.

Remembering. The act or process of bringing back to mind some information or content stored in one's **memory.** Since we can seem to remember events that may or may not have actually occurred, remembering appears to be an unreliable source of knowledge. Alternatively, genuine remembering could be defined as recalling events that have actually occurred, in which case it would be necessary to distinguish cases of genuine remembering from cases of (merely) apparent remembering.

Research programs. In the methodology of research programs elaborated by **Lakatos,** he suggests that the unit of science is neither the individual scientist, as **Popper** proposes, nor the entire community, as **Kuhn** maintains, but rather groups of scientists who pursue programs of research. See also **Lakatos, Imre; Kuhn, Thomas S.; Popper, Karl R.**

Rules. Patterns or regularities, descriptive or normative, that may have any number of instances. One of the most ambiguous words that occurs in philosophical discourse, the term "rule," can be used to refer to any custom, practice, or tradition; any habit, convention, or law; or any algorithm, principle, or heuristic, where the content of that rule can be specified in relation to conditions and responses, behavior, or outcomes under those conditions. Semantic rules, such as dictionary definitions, specify the meaning of words, but there are innumerable other kinds.

Rules of inference. Both deductive and inductive reasoning are governed by rules of inference, which specify what follows from what (in the case of deductive rules), and what supports what (in the case of inductive rules). A familiar deductive rule of inference is **modus ponens.** According to this rule, given "if *p* then *q*" and "*p*," infer "*q*," where the conclusion cannot be false if the premises are true. A familiar inductive rule of inference is *the straight rule,* also referred to as **induction by enumeration:** if *m/n* observed As have been Bs, infer that *m/n* As are Bs, when a large number of As have been observed over a wide variety of conditions. But such a conclusion can be false even when its premises are true. There are other important differences between rules of these kinds. See also **argument; inference.**

Russell, Bertrand (1872–1970). British mathematician and philosopher, who wrote prolifically on the central problems of epistemology, philosophy of science, and other central areas of philosophical inquiry. His *Principia Mathematica,* co-authored with A. N. Whitehead, is viewed as among the most important works on the foundations of mathematics. He is famous for his theory of proper names as **definite descriptions** and noted as an advocate of **logical atomism,** which he later repudiated. See also **knowledge by acquaintance vs. knowledge by description.**

S

Salmon, Wesley C. (1925–). American philosopher of science at the University of Pittsburgh, best known for his work on induction, including the problem of induction, and explanation, especially the statistical relevance model. See also **explanation, statistical relevance model of; induction, the problem of; vindication, pragmatic.**

Science. Formal science is the study of formal systems, while empirical science aims at the discovery of laws and theories. The former is or appears to be an **a priori** and **analytic** pursuit; the latter is or appears to be an **a posteriori** and **synthetic.** Empirical science may be described as aiming at the development of a model (theory) of the world, just as the **philosophy of science** might be described as aiming at the development of a model (explication) of science. But some contributions to science take the form of specific discoveries of particular phenomena (such as new planets, for example) that involve the application of laws and theories. See also **formal system; models/theories; theories, standard conception of.**

Scientism. The view that the only meaningful questions are those that are capable of being answered, under suitable conditions, by employing the methods of **empirical science.** Some versions insist this must be possible *in practice* (at present), while other versions submit that this should be possible *in principle* (at some past, present, or future time). Alternatively, the view that our only knowledge is produced by **science.**

Semantic entailment. A set of interpreted formulae of a **formal system** (the premises) semantically entails another interpreted formula (the conclusion) when the conclusion cannot be false if the premises are true. The construction of a formal system tends to be motivated by the desire to establish relations of **syntactic derivability** reflecting corresponding relations of semantic entailment. Within sentential logic, for example, an argument is syntactically valid if and only if its corresponding conditional—a conditional formed by taking the conjunction of its premises as its antecedent and its conclusion as its consequent—is a **tautology.**

Semantics. Study of relations between signs and what they stand for. Alternatively, the study of the relations between the formulae of an interpreted **formal system** and their meaning. Among the most important concepts studied within this area are those of meaning and of truth.

Semantics, possible-world. A semantic device for specifying the truth conditions for various types of intensional sentences, especially those of modal statements and of subjunctive conditionals, in relation to the properties of classes of possible worlds. While some theoreticians contend that possible worlds are "just as real" as the actual world, when properly understood, possible worlds are ways things might be or might have been as described by classes of sentences, where two worlds are the same possible world just in case they are described by all and only the same sentences. Those who believe that semantics can avoid possible worlds may overlook the distinction between *true* and *false,* where consistent sentences that are true describe ways things might be and are, whereas those that are false describe ways things might be and are not. Anytime we distinguish between the true and the false, therefore, we are distinguishing between different possible worlds and the actual one. The principal problem that confronts possible-world semantics is explaining which worlds are possible and why. Some of the most important contributions to this area have been made by Robert Stalnaker and by David Lewis.

Sense data/sense data theory. Sense data are the features of experience rather than of the things experienced. According to sense data theory, what we directly perceive in acts of perception are appearances of things. When real things are identified with the causes of appearances, the result is a **causal theory of perception.** When they are identified with constructions from appearances, the result is a **phenomenalistic theory of perception.**

Sentences/statements. A distinction is often drawn between sentences as grammatically well-formed formulae of a formal language and statements as sentences that are assigned specific interpretations in the absence of which they are neither true nor false. Thus, the members of the set of sentences fall into a syntactical category, while the members of the set of statements fall into a semantical category. These terms are frequently used more or less interchangeably to stand for syntactically well-formed formulae under an interpretation, even in the case of this glossary.

Sentential function (predicate expression). Any phrase or expression that can be turned into a sentence in four different ways. For example, if "Wx" means "x is made of wood," then by prefixing a *universal quantifier* "(x)" or an *existential quantifier* "(Ex)," either a universal generalization, "$(x)Wx$" ("Everything is made of wood"), or an existential generalization, "$(Ex)Wx$" ("Something is made of wood"), is generated. Or by replacing the occurrence of "x" by either an *individual constant* (or a proper name, say, "m" for "Madonna") or an *ambiguous name* (say, "a" for "Jane Doe"), two kinds of singular sentences

126

can be generated: "*Wm*" for "Madonna is made of wood" or "*Wa*" for "Jane Doe is made of wood," respectively. Ambiguous names are appropriate when either we do not know or do not want to identify whom we are taking about by name and when we are formalizing rules for generalizations that apply to everything, whether we have proper names for those things or not. See also **logic**.

Sentential logic. See **logic, sentential**.

Skepticism. The view that no one ever knows anything (global) or that no one ever knows what they think they know (local). Strictly speaking, there are as many versions of skepticism as there are notions of knowledge, but the strongest conceptions of knowledge—those incorporating a condition of certainty, for example—are most vulnerable to skepticism. See also **fallibilism; knowledge, classic conception of**.

Sociology of science. Any study of science that focuses on the practices of the members of the scientific community. Some students of the sociology of science, such as Robert Merton, study the sources of funding, the publication practices, and the professional organizations that tend to distinguish scientific activities. But other students, such as Barry Barnes and William Bloor, maintain that the sociology of science provides the only proper access route to understanding science. They investigate the causal conditions that affect the formation of beliefs in science as an alternative to theories of justification. See also **naturalized epistemology**.

Sound/soundness. A **formal system** is sound when every formula that is syntactically derivable as a theorem in that formal system is true of the abstract domain to which it applies. When it is also **complete,** the properties of semantic entailment and of syntactic derivability coincide. Alternatively, a **deductive argument** is sound when it is valid and its premises are true, in which case its conclusion cannot possibly be false.

Statements. Declarative sentences. Alternatively, what sentences assert to be the case. Frequently used as a synonym for **propositions.**

Subjunctive conditionals. See **conditionals.**

Symmetry thesis. According to Hempel's **covering-law model of explanation,** every adequate scientific explanation could have served as the basis for an adequate scientific prediction, had its premises been taken into account at a suitable time, and conversely. The relation between explanation and prediction is thus supposed to be symmetrical.

Syntactic derivability. A formula of a formal system is syntactically derivable from a set of formulae of a **formal system** (as premises) when it follows from those premises in accordance with an accepted rule of inference of that system. When those premises are *axioms* of the system, such a formula is said to be a *theorem*. Such rules of inference are formal insofar as their application depends exclusively upon the formal properties (of shape and size, etc.) of the marks that constitute (what is usually called) the vocabulary of that system, without concern for possible interpretations that make those formulae meaningful or true. The construction of a formal system, however, is normally motivated by the desire to reflect corresponding relations of **semantic entailment** with respect to the objects and relations of some abstract or physical domain.

Syntax. The study of the relations that signs bear to other signs, including how signs can be combined to produce new signs, especially with respect to their sizes, shapes, and other characteristics. With respect to language, syntax tends to be identified with grammar and semantics tends to be identified with meaning. Among the most important concepts of syntax is that of a *well-formed formula*, which is any sequence of marks from the vocabulary of a specified system of signs that satisfies the formation rules of that system. Thus, the *formation rules* specify which sequences of marks are formulae (or "sentences") of that system (or "language"). The *transformation rules* (for example, **modus ponens** and **modus tollens**) specify which formulae follow from which other formulae. Some syntactical systems are studied as **formal systems** relative to an abstract domain without concern for their possible interpretation in relation to some physical domain that might render those formulae meaningful assertions about the world. When this is the case, the notion of truth is displaced by that of theoremhood, where a formula of a formal system is a theorem of the system if it is derivable from that system's axioms. The crucial questions relating formal systems and abstract interpretations concern **soundness** and **completeness**. See also **theories, standard conception of.**

Synthetic a priori knowledge. See also **analytic/ synthetic distinction; a priori/a posteriori distinction; Kant, I.; rationalism.**

T

Tarski, Alfred (1902–   ). Polish-American mathematician and philosopher, noted for his work on formal methods, especially the semantic conception of truth. See also **semantics; truth, the semantic conception of.**

Tautology. In its narrow sense, any **logical truth.** In a broader sense, any analytic sentence. See also **analytic/ synthetic distinction.**

Testability. See **cognitive significance.**

Theist/theism. An advocate of the thesis that belief in the existence of God is rationally justified. Alternatively, anyone who believes in the existence of God, whether or not they have any good reasons. While God has been envisioned as a Supreme Being who created the universe, different forms of theism result from the very conception in which one believes. *Pantheism,* for example, identifies God with nature, in which case evidence for the existence of nature is evidence for the existence of God. *Deism* identifies God with the creator of the universe, but who left the world, once created, to its own devices. *Polytheism* identifies not one but many gods, who may possess unequal powers and responsibilities and intervene in human affairs. Traditional *monotheism* holds that there is one and only one Supreme Being who is all knowing (omniscient), all powerful (omnipotent), and all good (omnibenevolent). The difficulty encountered in reconciling this conception of God with a world that includes plagues, wars, pestilence, famine, etc., is known as *the problem of evil.* See also **agnostic/agnosticism; atheist/ atheism.**

Theories. Any conjecture or hypothesis, especially one that has yet to be confirmed, is customarily described as (only) "a theory." Philosophical explications are also sometimes called "theories." Alternatively, any conjecture or hypothesis in science, no matter whether it is confirmed or not. See also **theories, scientific.**

Theories, Hempel's conception of. As an alternative to the standard conception of scientific theories, Hempel has proposed the view of theories as consisting of *internal principles* and *bridge principles.* A theory's internal principles are the theory's distinctive hypotheses (which might be couched in observational or theoretical language), while its bridge principles provide a means for relating the theory's assertions to previously understood language, background knowledge, and auxiliary hypotheses. This concept does not depend upon the analytic/synthetic distinction or even the observable/theoretical distinction. See also **theories, standard conception of.**

Theories, scientific. The discovery of universal explanatory theories is often taken to be the aim of science. This can be reconciled with the idea that science aims at discovering laws of nature when theories are envisioned as sets of laws that apply to a common domain. Making this notion more precise has proven difficult, and some accounts envision theories as entities that do not appeal to laws. The principal theories about theories currently include **the standard conception, Hempel's** later **conception,** and **the semantic conception.** Among the most important disputes about scientific theories is the status of theoretical entities, which divides realists and instrumentalists.

Theories, semantic conception of. The most recent account of the nature of scientific theories has been advanced in various forms by Patrick Suppes, Joseph Sneed, and Frederick Suppe, among others, building on the earlier work of E. W. Beth. In its simplest versions, scientific theories consist of *theoretical definitions* that define theoretical predicates, where *empirical hypotheses* might relate those predicates to specific portions of the world. Ronald Giere, for example, has suggested that theoretical predicates might define different kinds of systems, where a *classical particle system* can be defined as a system that obeys Newton's three laws of motion and inverse-square law of universal gravitation. The empirical hypothesis can then be asserted that the Sun and planets of our solar system constitute a classical particle system. Advocates of the semantic conception, however, differ greatly in their attitudes about laws of nature. Some view them as counterfactual idealizations, while others dispense with them altogether.

Theories, standard conception of. The standard conception views theories as *abstract calculi* conjoined with *empirical interpretations*. Thus, they are formal systems that describe the world. An example would be the difference between empirically uninterpreted Euclidean geometry and empirically interpreted Euclidean geometry, where the lines and points of pure geometry become features of applied geometry by identifying lines with paths of light rays and points with their intersections in space. Once a **formal system** has been given an empirical interpretation, it then becomes empirically testable. The **observable/theoretical distinction** and the **analytic/ synthetic distinction** are assumed. Theoretical laws are generalizations whose non-logical terms are exclusively theoretical. Empirical laws are generalizations whose non-logical terms are exclusively observational. A scientific theory thus consists of theoretical laws and *correspondence rules,* which relate theoretical laws and observable phenomena by employing a mixed non-logical vocabulary. An empirical law might therefore be explained by its derivation from that theory. The standard conception has been attacked by denying the adequacy of the distinctions that it takes for granted, especially by proponents of the **semantic conception.**

Theories, underdetermination of. The thesis that the content of a scientific theory is always greater than its set of empirically testable consequences, which implies that theories, however testable, are never conclusively verifiable. A special instance of this thesis, which has also been advanced by **W. V. O. Quine,** is known as the **indeterminacy of translation.**

Total evidence, requirement of. This requirement specifies that, in the process of applying inductive inference rules, the premises must describe all of the available relevant evidence. Some relevant evidence, of course, may not be available, and some available evidence may not be relevant. The appropriate concept of relevance is one of evidential relevance, where a sentence S is *evidentially relevant* to an hypothesis h if and only if the truth or the falsity of S makes a difference to the truth or the falsity of h. Theories of confirmation may be viewed as attempts to render this notion more precise. The importance of this requirement is emphasized by Rudolf Carnap, but some thinkers have misunderstood it as a demand that every item of knowledge currently available has to be included in the premises of a proper inductive argument, which is false.

Transcendental argument. A species of argument that maintains that any proposition that is a necessary precondition for beliefs that are universally accepted as true must also be true. For example, it could be argued that, since everyone acknowledges that the existence of objective or correct answers to questions is a necessary condition for the successful conduct of inquiry, objective or correct answers to questions have to exist. In this form, transcendental arguments may sometimes appear to take for granted issues that really ought to be established on independent ground and thereby beg the question. Alternatively, any argument in support of conclusions about the conditions that must be satisfied for any knowledge to be possible at all. As pursued by Kant, for example, a transcendental argument is given for the existence of the

Forms of Intuition and the Categories of Experience as necessary conditions of experience. See also **Kant, I.**

Translation, indeterminacy of. The thesis that the meaning of a language can never be translated with complete determinacy, because the evidence for its meaning never exhausts that meaning. Advanced by **W. V. O. Quine,** this thesis is a special case of the underdetermination of theories by empirical evidence. See also **theories, underdetermination of.**

Truth, coherence theory of. Defines "true" as a property of sets of beliefs that are mutually reinforcing (or "hang together") while satisfying conditions of logical consistency (where it is not the case that, for any belief b, both b and its negation, not-b, are accepted at the same time) and of deductive closure (where, if the truth of belief $b1$ logically requires the truth of belief $b2$, then $b2$ must also be accepted whenever $b1$ is accepted). Since one person at two different times or two persons at the same time are entitled to completely different beliefs as long as their belief sets are coherent, the coherence theory does not entail the correspondence theory.

Truth conditions. Any necessary or sufficient conditions for a sentence, statement, or proposition to be true. The sentence, "Mary is smart," for example, would be true if and only if the person named by the name "Mary" has the property described by the predicate "is smart." Truth conditions for molecular sentences can be readily constructed from those for atomic sentences when those molecular sentences are extensional (truth functional); otherwise their truth conditions will have to be determined. A distinction is usually drawn between truth and confirmation, but pragmatic theories tend to blur the difference. See also **logic; ontic/epistemic; truth, pragmatic conception of; truth, semantic conception of.**

Truth, correspondence theory of. Defines "true" as designating the property of a declarative sentence when what it asserts to be the case is the case. Such a sentence ("John is a bachelor") is true when the world (or **reality**) is the way it is thereby described as being or when that sentence "corresponds" to the world (because, in this case, John is a bachelor). The semantic theory of truth is a refinement of the correspondence theory.

Truth, criteria of. The appropriate standards of evidence that, if satisfied, entitle us to believe that something is true. Alternatively, criteria of truth are the **acceptance and rejection rules** specified by a theory of knowledge. See also **criteria, the problem of; epistemology.**

Truth, Peircean theory of. Defines "true" as a property of those beliefs that the community of inquirers is ultimately destined to accept or to agree upon in the long run (that is, the opinion that they will share in common as a result of applying scientific methods to answerable questions concerning the world forever). Alternatively, it is the opinion that they *would* share if they *were* to apply scientific methods to answerable questions concerning the world forever. In either formulation, those beliefs are thought to "correspond" to the world. Strictly speaking, truth in Peirce's sense does not guarantee correspondence. In the meanwhile, rational beliefs are those whose acceptance is suitably warranted by the available relevant evidence.

Truth, pragmatic theory of. Defines "true" as designating the property a declarative sentence has when its assertion (or acceptance) is fully warranted. This requires that the available evidence is sufficient to justify its assertion (or acceptance). Yet it differs from the correspondence theory insofar as sentences whose assertion is fully warranted might not describe (or "correspond to") the world. See also **truth, correspondence theory of.**

Truth, redundancy theory of. Asserts that the word "true" has no unique or special function within language and can be eliminated without thereby limiting the expressive adequacy of a language. Sentences that appeal to truth (such as "It is true that Queen Anne is dead") have exactly the same content as others that do not (such as "Queen Anne is dead"). It thus implies that the role of assertions of truth at best is merely to emphasize what is being asserted and at worst is simply redundant, which in turn suggests that there is no problem of truth and no need for a theory of truth.

Truth, regulative notion of. Maintains that, whether or not any declarative sentence ever satisfies the correspondence definition of truth, the objective of attaining truth envisioned as correspondence can still function as a regulative ideal for the process of inquiry and thereby encourage us to satisfy suitable standards of rationality. See also **truth, Peircean theory of.**

Truth, semantic conception of. Maintains that truth ought to be interpreted as a metalinguistic predicate in order to avoid various semantic paradoxes (such as the sentence that asserts of itself, "This sentence is false," which is true if it is false and false if it is true). Truth is viewed as a predicate that occurs in a **metalanguage** to describe sentences that occur in an **object-language.** Truth ascriptions are relative to a language and require adequate translations in the language in which they are expressed. The sentence, "'Schnee ist weiss' is true in German if and only if snow is white," thus specifies necessary and sufficient conditions of truth for the sentence "Schnee ist weiss" in German provided that it is properly translated within the meta-language of English by the sentence "Snow is white." In his technical papers, **Alfred Tarski** has shown how this view can be generalized for languages of certain formal kinds as a special case of the correspondence theory of truth.

Truth, theories of. See **truth, coherence theory of; truth, correspondence theory of; truth, Peircean theory of; truth, pragmatic theory of; truth, redundancy theory of; truth, semantic conception of.**

Truth, vacuous. Characterizes any theory or definition of truth that cannot be ascertained to have any instances in relation to reasonable standards of evidence, for example, "Truth is God's will." Alternatively, sentences that are true and remain true under all interpretations of their non-logical components as logical truths are "vacuous" by virtue of having zero content.

Truth vs. confirmation. See **confirmation vs. truth.**

U

Uncertainty. The mental state of non-belief; the opposite of believing or dis-believing. Alternatively, lack of conviction; the opposite of **certainty.**

Uniform interpretation, requirement of. In translating an argument into formal syntax or in applying a formal rule of inference, every occurrence of the same syntactical sign must be assigned the same (or a "uniform") interpretation. In applying the deductive rule of inference **modus ponens,** "Given 'if p then q' and 'p,' infer q," for example, the same variables (here, "p" and "q") must be uniformly replaced by the same specific sentences. Thus, if "p" stands for "John is a bachelor" in the first instance, then it must also stand for "John is a bachelor" in the second instance, and similarly for "*q.*" This requirement not only blocks the commission of various fallacies but also suggests how the construction of syntactical systems, including rules of inference, is determined by considerations of semantics.

Universal generalization. Any generalization of the form, "All As are Bs" or, more generally, any sentence that attributes some property or its absence to every member of a reference class. See also **conditionals; existential generalization; laws of nature.**

Universal vs. commensurately universal properties. Aristotle drew a distinction between the universal and the commensurately universal properties of things (*Posterior Analytics* I, 73a–74a). (Merely) universal properties are properties that everything of a certain kind happens to have but could continue to exist without, commensurately universal properties that everything of a certain kind has and that nothing of that kind could continue to exist without. Indeed, for Aristotle, commensurately universal properties are essential properties, which occur in a proper definition of things of that kind. (Merely) universal properties, by comparison, are only accidental and not definitional. See also **Aristotle; laws of nature.**

Universals. Universals are properties that can have any number of instances. Alternatively, any property that, in principle, could be attributed to (or "predicated of") any member of any possible world. According to nominalism, there is no more to universals than their classes of instances. See also **nominalism vs. realism.**

V

Verifiability. Broadly speaking, a sentence is verifiable when, under suitable conditions, it could be shown to be true (probably true). Strictly speaking, however, a sentence is verifiable when it is not analytic but is deducible from a logically consistent, finite set of sentences that describe the results of possible observations and experiments. Different classes of sentences can be verified or falsified. For example, existential generalizations are verifiable but not falsifiable, while universal generalizations are falsifiable but not verifiable. Logical positivism embraced verifiability as a criterion of meaningfulness for separating sentences that were meaningful from those that were not. See also **falsifiability; meaningfulness, problem of; verifiability criterion of meaningfulness.**

Verifiability criterion of meaningfulness. The principle that a sentence is meaningful (cognitively significant, not nonsense) only if its truth is subject to verification. Although originally intended to separate meaningless metaphysical assertions from genuinely meaningful hypotheses, this standard qualifies sentences with universal scope (including lawlike hypotheses); sentences of mixed quantification (such as every metal has a melting point), and sentences appealing to infinite sequences (such as probability hypotheses under the frequency interpretation) as meaningless. The verifiability criterion of meaning was embraced by **logical positivism** but rejected by **logical empiricism.** But the **problem of meaningfulness** must be differentiated from the **problem of demarcation.**

Verification. Broadly speaking, an hypothesis is subject to verification by the discovery of any evidence that supports or confirms its truth. Strictly speaking, *verification* is the process of establishing the truth of a sentence by deducing it from a logically consistent, finite set of sentences that describe the results of actual observations and experiments, especially when observational sentences are taken to be incorrigible. Likewise, *falsification* is the process of establishing the falsity of a sentence by the same method. If observation sentences are fallible, then no synthetic sentences turn out to be verifiable or falsifiable in an absolute sense, even if, in a relative sense, they may still be viewed as verifiable or falsifiable in relation to other observation sentences whose truth is taken for granted.

Verisimilitude. Refers to the truthlikeness of an hypothesis or theory, where truthlikeness represents degree of truth (or approximate truth). In defense of certain views about the growth of scientific knowlege, such as those of **Popper,** for example, criteria of verisimilitude are important.

Vindication, pragmatic. A solution to the problem of induction by attempting to demonstrate that the method of science is capable of attaining its goal, if any method is capable of attaining that goal, when that method and that goal are properly conceived. Advocated by **Hans Reichenbach** and by **Wesley C. Salmon,** the goal of science is envisioned as the discovery of limiting frequencies within infinite sequences and the method of science is envisioned as based upon the **principle of induction by enumeration.** The pragmatic vindication is the argument that, if the method of science, thus conceived, were to be relied upon forever, the goal of science, thus conceived, would eventually be achieved, necessarily, provided that those limiting frequencies exist. It does not establish that this goal can actually be attained, however, since those limiting frequencies may not exist. What it purports to establish, therefore, is the more modest claim that, when properly understood, scientific method can attain the goal of science if any method can.

Virtue epistemology. A form of **reliabilism** that views knowledge as true beliefs that arise from cognitive virtue, which is an ability or a competence to arrive at truths and to avoid falsehoods within a specific domain of inquiry.

W

Why-questions, explanation seeking. A why-question that asks why an event or occurrence described by an explanandum sentence has taken place or requests information concerning the laws and conditions that brought it about. Two alternative desiderata that adequate answers to questions of this kind might have to satisfy are those of **nomic expectability** and of **nomic responsibility.**

Why-questions, reason seeking. A why-question that asks why a sentence that describes an event or occurrence should be accepted as true and requests information concerning the evidence that supports the conclusion that that sentence is true. Two alternative desiderata that adequate answers to questions of this kind might have to satisfy are those of the requirement of total evidence and the requirement of maximal specificity. See also **explanation, covering-law model of.**

Selected Bibliography

Among the most important journals publishing articles in epistemology and the philosophy of science are *American Philosophical Quarterly; British Journal for Philosophy of Science; Erkenntnis; Journal of Philosophy; Nous; Philosophical Studies; Philosophy of Science; and Synthese.* For additional references, please consult your instructor or a librarian.

The following books are recommended for study, not because they are classics in the field (although some of them are), but because they have proven to be useful to other students of epistemology and philosophy of science. They fall into three categories in terms of their level of difficulty, identified here as "elementary," "somewhat difficult," and "advanced."

Ackermann, Robert. *Theories of Knowledge: A Critical Introduction.* New York: McGraw-Hill Book Company, 1965. Combines selections from Plato, Aristotle, Descartes, Berkeley, Hume, Kant, and Peirce with excellent discussions of their views. Elementary.

Almeder, Robert. *Blind Realism: An Essay on Human*

Knowledge and Natural Science. Lanham, MD: Rowman and Littlefield, 1991. Offers an introduction to the theory of knowledge and a defense of blind realism. Somewhat difficult.

Ayer, Alfred J. *The Problem of Knowledge*. Harmondsworth, UK: Penguin Books, 1956. (Paperback) A valuable introduction to the theory of knowledge by the author of *Language, Truth and Logic*, which virtually defined logical positivism. Elementary.

Chalmers, Alan F. *What Is This Thing Called Science?* Atlantic Highlands, NJ: The Humanities Press, 1976. (Paperback) A very lucid and accessible introduction to the philosophy of science emphasizing theories of the growth of scientific knowledge. Elementary.

Fetzer, James H. *Philosophy of Science*. New York: Paragon, 1993. (Paperback) An introduction to the history and philosophy of science that emphasizes the problem of developing an adequate theory of the nature of laws of nature. Elementary.

Goodman, Nelson. *Fact, Fiction and Forecast*. Cambridge: Harvard University Press, 1983. 4th edition. (Paperback) A classic in the philosophy of science, this work raises fascinating problems about counterfactuals, dispositions, and laws. Somewhat difficult.

Hempel, Carl G. *Aspects of Scientific Explanation*. New York: The Free Press, 1965. (Paperback) An invaluable collection of the most important papers by one of the most influential philosophers of science of the twentieth century. Somewhat difficult.

Hintikka, Jaakko. *Knowledge and Belief*. Ithaca: Cornell University Press, 1962. An influential work that brings modern logic to bear upon the formalization of epistemic relations by means of axioms and theorems. Advanced.

Humphreys, Paul. *The Chances of Explanation*. Princeton: Princeton University Press, 1990. (Paperback) A sophisticated study of explanation and problems of causation in the social, medical, and physical sciences. Advanced.

Kitcher, Philip, and Wesley C. Salmon, eds. *Scientific Explanation*. Minneapolis: University of Minnesota Press, 1989. (Paperback) An excellent collection of recent articles on the nature of scientific explanation and related issues, including a survey of the history of work in this field by Salmon. Somewhat difficult.

Kornblith, Hilary, ed. *Naturalizing Epistemology*. Cambridge: MIT Press, 1985. (Paperback) A valuable collection of papers by various authors, including W. V. O. Quine, who favor one or another version of naturalized epistemology. Somewhat difficult.

Kuhn, Thomas S. *The Structure of Scientific Revolutions*. Chicago: University of Chicago Press, 1964. (Paperback) One of the most influential works of recent times, this book has created a revolution of its own in the history and philosophy of science. Somewhat difficult.

Kyburg, Henry, and Howard Smokler, eds. *Studies in Subjective Probabililty*. Huntington, NY: Krieger Publishing Company, 2nd edition, 1980. (Paperback) An excellent collection of source materials on subjective approaches to probability and induction. Advanced.

Lakatos, Imre, and Alan Musgrave, eds. *Criticism and the Growth of Scientific Knowledge*. Cambridge, UK: Cambridge University Press, 1971. An invaluable collection of brilliant studies on scientific methodology by some of the most important thinkers. Somewhat difficult.

Leplin, Jarrett, ed. *Scientific Realism*. Berkeley, CA: University of California Press, 1984. (Paperback) An excellent collection of papers on one of the most important problems in the philosophy of science by representatives of different views. Somewhat difficult.

Morick, Harold, ed. *Challenges to Empiricism*. Belmont, CA: Wadsworth Publishing Company, 1972. (Paperback) A valuable collection of articles presenting fascinating alternatives to classic forms of empiricism. Varies from elementary to somewhat difficult.

Pappas, George, and Marshall Swain, eds. *Essays on Knowledge and Justification*. Ithaca: Cornell University Press, 1978. (Paperback) A valuable collection of articles on different aspects of the theory of knowledge by contemporary philosophers. Somewhat difficult.

Pollock, John. *Contemporary Theories of Knowledge*. Savage, MD: Rowman and Littlefield, 1986. (Paperback) A survey of various approaches to the theory of knowledge, including foundations theories, coherence theories, externalism, and internalism. Somewhat difficult.

Popper, Karl R. *Conjectures and Refutations*. New York: Harper & Row, 1968. (Paperback) This is the best collection of essays by one of the most influential figures in the philosophy of science of the twentieth century. Varies from elementary to somewhat difficult.

Reichenbach, Hans. *Experience and Prediction*. Chicago: University of Chicago Press, 1938. A brilliant presentation of the worldview of a Humean frequentist, who views science as providing the most rational basis for anticipating the course of experience. Elementary.

Rorty, Richard. *Philosophy and the Mirror of Nature*. Princeton: Princeton University Press, 1979. (Paperback) A very sophisticated and controversial study of the nature of science, knowledge, and rationality by a contemporary pragmatist. Somewhat difficult.

Russell, Bertrand. *Human Knowledge: Its Scope and Limits*. New York: Simon and Schuster, 1948. (Paperback) Russell, who won a Nobel Prize for literature (there is none in philosophy), provides an excellent discussion of major issues in the theory of knowledge. Elementary.

Salmon, Wesley C. *The Foundation of Scientific Inference.* Pittsburgh, PA: University of Pittsburgh Press, 1965. (Paperback) An illuminating survey of basic concepts of probability and induction that emphasizes the problem of induction. Elementary.

Scheffler, Israel. *Conditions of Knowledge.* Chicago: University of Chicago, 1965. (Paperback) An extremely lucid survey of variations on the traditional conception of knowledge, related to the goals of education. Varies from elementary to somewhat difficult.

Skyrms, Brian. *Choice & Chance: An Introduction to Inductive Logic,* Belmont, CA: Wadsworth Publishing Company, 1986. 3rd edition. A very lucid introduction to basic concepts of probability and induction by a Bayesian personalist. Elementary.

Suppe, Fred, ed. *The Structure of Scientific Theories.* Urbana: University of Illinois Press, 2nd edition, 1977. (Paperback) Everything you ever wanted to know about theories about theories, including a defense of the semantic approach. Somewhat difficult.

Tuana, Nancy, ed. *Feminism & Science.* Bloomington: Indiana University Press, 1989. (Paperback) A valuable collection of studies on the relations and connections between feminism and science by more than a dozen feminist philosophers. Somewhat difficult.

About the Authors

James H. Fetzer is Professor of Philosophy at the University of Minnesota, Duluth. He is the author of *Scientific Knowledge* (1981); *AI: Its Scope and Limits* (1990); *Philosophy and Cognitive Science* (1991); and *Philosophy of Science* (1993); as well as the editor or co-editor of eleven other books, including *Principles of Philosophical Reasoning* (1984); *Probability and Causality* (1988); *Definitions and Definability* (1991); and *Foundations of Philosophy of Science: Recent Developments* (1993). He is editor of *Minds and Machines,* co-editor of *Synthese,* and series editor of *Studies in Cognitive Systems.* He has published more than seventy articles and reviews.

Robert F. Almeder is Professor of Philosophy at Georgia State University. He is the author of *Charles S. Peirce: A Critical Introduction* (1980); *Blind Realism: An Essay on Human Knowledge and Natural Science* (1991); and two other books. He is also the editor of *Praxis and Reason: Studies in the Philosophy of Nicholas Rescher* (1982) and the co-editor of ten other books. He has served as President of the Charles S. Peirce Society (1980) and received the Outstanding Educator of America Award (1983). He has also authored more than sixty articles and reviews for professional journals and books.